Institutional Units

Institutional Units:
Performance and Efficiency Measurement

Dr Rangalal Mohapatra

KALPAZ

First Published, 2018

Published by

Kalpaz Publications
C-30, Satyawati Nagar,
Delhi – 110052
E-mail: kalpaz@hotmail.com
Ph.: 9212142040

Printed at: G. Print Process, Delhi

Cataloging in Publication Data—DK
Courtesy: D.K. Agencies (P) Ltd. <docinfo@dkagencies.com>

Mohapatra, Rangalal, author.
Institutional units : performance and efficiency measurement / Dr Rangalal Mohapatra.
pages cm
Includes bibliographical references.
ISBN 9789386397515 (HB)

1. Sikkim University—Evaluation. 2. Sikkim University.—Ratings and rankings. 3. Education, Higher—India—Gangtok—Evaluation. 4. Data envelopment analysis—India—Gangtok. I. Title.

LCC LB2331.65.I4M64 2018 | DDC 378.954167 23

Contents

Foreword

I am happy to write a few lines of appreciation of the book written by Dr Rangalal Mohapatra of Sikkim University. This book is the outcome of a research project sponsored by the Sikkim University itself. The University should also be complemented for coming forward to have a transparent and objective evaluation of the functioning of its various academic departments, by an evaluator who is a part and parcel of the University fraternity.

At a juncture when the public funded higher educational institutions in the country lost sight of accountability and quality of education, the various reforms of recent times in the sphere of higher educational sector should be viewed as a paradigmic shift. With expansion of higher educational institutions, rise in enrolment and globally competitive environment, the need of the hour has been an emphasis on accountability, cost-effectiveness and quality of education. To implement these ideas, a periodic, objective and detailed assessment of the institutions becomes necessary. For undertaking such an exercise, a set of measurable parameters covering inputs as well as outputs should be scientifically identified. Further, a micro-level assessment should be done, as educational institutions across, having common objectives and goals, may not always be comparable. Dr Rangalal Mohapatra's work should be seen in this context. He made a detailed evaluation of the functioning of various units of the University by gathering information on various inputs and outputs and scientifically analysed the same. The methodology adopted is the state-of-the-art Data Envelopment Analysis which is quite popular for analysing relative efficiency of decision-making units. The modelling methodology has been tried out with various input and output combinations, and also department combinations. The book has finally come out successfully with measures of relative efficiency of the various departments of the Sikkim University. The novelty of the book is a microlevel detailed examination of a University which should be taken as a role model for other higher educational institutions in the country.

This work embodied in this book is highly commendable and would serve as a guide book to researchers wanting to evaluate similar institutions.The finding are also useful to the educational administrators to have an overall social audit of the human capital formation to reap the demographic dividend in a globalising world. The book is also useful to the academia, educational planners and the general perceptible readers.

On the whole, the book is a welcome addition to the scantily available research work in this area. I personally congratulate Dr Rangalal Mohapatra who is a devoted research economist, to have undertaken work in this area and make the findings available in the form of this book.

I wish him all the best.

Bandi Kamaiah

Preface

Accountability, value for money, cost effectiveness, transparency and moreover, measurement of organisational efficiency is recognised as an integral part of implementation, monitoring and constant evaluation irrespective of the nature of the organisation whether profitable or non profitable. Higher education sector of many countries especially the universities obtain some of their public funds making it essential in the interest of accountability, to measure the efficiency of institutions which comprise these sectors. Over the past few years, India's Higher Education sector has witnessed tremendous growth. Today the country has the largest education system in the world in terms of the number of institutions, second in terms of enrolment. Improving the efficiency of educational systems is a growing concern of educational planners and academicians in the recent years. The key concern for India is the creation of an employable workforce to harness its demographic dividend to maximum extent. Improving ***Skill, Speed and Scale*** at micro-unit level in the higher educational institutions especially in the universities of National character must be focused to achieve the development agenda of ***inclusive growth of all.***

The development of high technology have major consequences for higher education and have been responsible for transforming it into a key instrument of economic development and it has transformed Higher Education Institutions (HEI) into private market and performance driven competing university-as-firms. This has involved application of business principles and management processes, with a strong emphasis on accountability, transparency and performances. Because higher education plays a fundamental role in creating competitive advantage in a market environment, performance matters. Therefore, the objectives of HEI settle into two related objectives: (i) maximising the capacity and performance within the global landscape, and (ii) optimising benefits of the linkages of national and local settings (Van der Wende, 2009).

There is a growing consciousness with the university ranking around the world. Started as an academic exercise in the early twentieth century, it became a 'commercial' information service for the students in 1980's resulting into a situation of reputation race with geographical implication. This ranking consciousness became more serious in response to globalisation and the pursuit of new knowledge as the basis of economic growth, and the drive for increased public accountability and transparency. Ranking has become the "*Battle for Excellence*" and determines the status of the individual institutions and gauge its global competitiveness. In this process, rankings of the universities are transforming and reshaping higher education system.

In this context, interest on the performance on higher education has become a burning issue for the academicians and policy makers. In higher education, productivity improvement is seen as the most promising strategy for containing costs in the continuing effort to keep higher education affordable. Hence, concepts such as productivity and efficiency and accountability are central to the sustainability, cost and quality of higher education.

Data Envelopment Analysis (DEA) is the term coined in the operation research literature by Charnes, Cooper and Rhodes (CCR-1978) to measure the technical efficiency of a given observed Decision Making Unit (DMU) assuming CRS production technology for multi-input and multi-output correspondence. Further, Banker, Charnes and Cooper (1984) extended it to analyse decomposition of technical and scale efficiency using VRS (Variable Returns to Scale) technology.

The most significant literature on educational production using DEA is Banker and Morey (1986) which allowed Non-Discretionary inputs. Since efficiency lies at the forefront of policy debates around restructuring of the educational institutions' functioning, study of efficiency of the university at departmental level is a necessity. In order to estimate the efficiency of individual departments of Sikkim University as proposed in the proposal, the data on inputs and outputs of each department have been collected.

The book has been divided into five main chapters. Chapter-1 briefly explains the importance of higher education to economic growth and the importance of ranking of universities and thereby the necessity of measuring the efficiency of the departments functioning in the university. This chapter after giving a brief survey of the literature on measuring efficiency of educational institutions outlines the objectives of the study, the type sources and the nature of the data. The first chapter ends with small hints about the methods of analysis employed in the study.

Hence, the Second Chapter discusses about the theoretical background of Efficiency evaluation. The chapter deals with the meaning of efficiency, types of efficiency and the methods available to measure the efficiency level. The last section brings out the CCR and BCC model of DEA and The Concept of Super Efficiency to rank the fully efficient units that could not be assigned distinct number other than 1.

The Third Chapter is on the detail discussion of the concept of university, university education in India, initiatives by UGC on higher education in India, about the Sikkim University, its structure and position. The fourth chapter is about the analysis and interpretation of the results department-wise for CCR and BCC model. Fifth Chapter deals with the Super Efficiency Model and the results and interpretation.

It is hoped that this book will be useful for those engaged in research and applications of operations research and performance measurement (including those who work in the field of economics). DEA is likely to be offered as a full course or as part of advanced quantitative courses in the departments of Business Management, Science, Quantitative Techniques, Industrial Engineering, Industrial Management or Mathematics of many universities and institutions. With the growing numbers of basic and advanced courses on DEA in many universities and institutions across the world, including the USA, Europe and Asia, it is expected that the book will have a good audience, including students, researchers and practicing consultants, engaged in operations research and performance measurement.

Acknowledgement

Many people have made important contributions to the development and completion of the book. I owe my special debt to Sikkim University for providing the full financial support for the present work in the form of a project. I express my gratitude to the then honourable Vice Chancellor Professor Tanka Bahadur Subba who had encouraged me to work on the project with full financial support of the Sikkim University, Central University of India.

I also express my deepest sense of gratitude to Dr. Suresh Gurung, the Joint Registrar, Academic, Sikkim University who personally inspired me to apply for the project as per the SikkimUniversity guidelines, without which, I would not have even applied for the project.

At the same time I must express my thankfulness to the Deans Committee on the selection and award of project, who has selected my proposal for the grant of award for the project.

I am highly indebted to Controller of Examination, Sikkim University and all the personnel of the Examination department who have helped me a lot in providing all the data regarding students' examination marks etc. in time despite their busy schedule.

I acknowledge my deep sense of gratitude to Dr. Sailesh Kumar, Assistant Professor, Department of Management, Sikkim University, who without any hesitation allowed me to use his name as the co-investigator of the project. Even though he could not do anything for the project during the project period still he allowed me to put his name without which the project proposal could not have been accepted as two persons were required for the project application. However, I am grateful to him forever for his support to me for this work.

I must express my gratefulness to Professor B Kamaiah Emeritus Professor of Economics, University of Hyderabad and Professor Bhabesh Sen, Professor in Economics, XIBM, Bhubaneswar, (Ex. Professor, A & A Economics, Utkal University) whose constant inspiration during my studentship is immensely useful and beneficial. Their constant encouragement and support has helped me to reach at this stage.

I must express my special thanks to Registrar, Finance Department, Sikkim University and the Establishment Department, Sikkim University for their help in processing the file and sanctioning the money in the time of need without any difficulty. Above all, the cordial supports of all the administrative personnel of Sikkim University are acknowledged with deep sense of gratitude.

I must express my special gratitude to Mr. Amit Garg of Kalpaz Publications and his team for accepting my proposal to publish it in the book form. His timely response and quick action helped me making my work worthy of publication.

Lastly, I must express my heartfelt thanksgiving to my wife Mrs. **Nirupama Mohapatra** and my only daughter **Neeraja Mohapatra** who have constantly supported and encouraged me both mentally and physically all the time to come up with this work.

List of Abbreviations

AE	: Allocative Efficiency
BCC	: Banker, Charnes and Cooper
CCR	: Charnes Cooper and Rhodes
C-D	: Cobb Douglas
CRS	: Constant Returns to Scale
CUS	: Central University of Sikkim
DEA	: Data Envelopment Analysis
DMU	: Decision Making Unit
GER	: Gross Enrolment Ratio
GOI	: Government of India
HEI	: Higher Education Institutions
IRS	: Increasing Returns to Scale
ICT	: Information and Communication Technology
MHRD	: Ministry of Human Resource and Development
MOLS	: Modified Ordinary Least Square
MPSS	: Most Productive Scale and Size
NAAC	: National Assessment and Accreditation Council
OE	: Overall Efficiency
OLS	: Ordinary Least Square
PG	: Post Graduate
POA	: Programme of Action

SBM : Slack Based Measurement

SE : Super Efficiency

SFA : Stochastic Frontier Analysis

TE : Technical Efficiency

UG : Under Graduate

UGC : University Grant, Commission

VRS : Variable Returns to Scale

List of Equations

Equation-1: $Ln(y_i) = \ln[f(x_{i1,} \dots \dots \dots \dots, x_{im})] - u_i$

Equation-2: $\frac{y_i}{f(x_{i1,} \quad x_{im}} = e^{-u}$

Equation-3: $Ln(y_i) = \ln[f(x_{i1,} \dots \dots \dots \dots, x_{im})] + \varepsilon_i$

Equation-4: $\ln L = -n \ln \sigma - \frac{n}{2} ln \frac{2}{\pi} - \frac{1}{2} \sum_i \ln \phi \left(\frac{-\varepsilon_i \lambda}{\sigma} \right)$

Equation-5: $E(u_i | \varepsilon_i) = \frac{\sigma_u \sigma_v}{\sigma} [\frac{\Phi(\varepsilon_i \lambda / \sigma)}{1 - \Phi(\varepsilon_i \lambda / \sigma)} - \frac{\varepsilon_i \lambda}{\sigma}$

Equation-6: $\frac{u_1 y_{10} + u_2 y_{20} +, \dots \dots + u_{sy}{}_{s0}}{v_1 x_{10} + v_2 x_{20} +, \dots \dots + v_m x_{m0}}$

Equation-7: $\underset{v,u}{Max} \quad \theta = \frac{u_1 y_{10} + u_2 y_{20} +, \dots \dots + u_{sy}{}_{s0}}{v_1 x_{10} + v_2 x_{20} +, \dots \dots + v_m x_{m0}}$

Equation-8: $\frac{u_1 y_{1j} +, \dots \dots u_s y_{sj}}{v_1 x_{1j} + \cdots \dots \dots v_m x_{mj}} \leq 1$

Equation-9: $\underset{\mu,v}{Max} \quad \theta = \mu_1 y_{10} +, \dots \dots \dots \dots \dots, \mu_s y_{so}$

Equation-10: $(\mathrm{LP_o}) \underset{v,u}{Max} \quad u\, y_o$

Equation-11: $\underset{\theta,\lambda}{min} \quad \theta \ subject\ to\ \theta x_o - X\lambda \leq 0$

Equation-12: $\underset{\lambda, s^- s^+}{Max} \quad w = es^- + es^+$

Equation-13: $\widehat{x}_o = \theta^* x_o - s^{-*} \leq x_o \ and\ \hat{y}_o = y_o + s^{+*} \geq y_o$

Equation-14: $\underset{\theta_{B,\lambda}}{Min} \quad \theta_B$

Equation-15: $DLPO_o = \underset{\eta,\mu}{\mathrm{Max}} \quad \eta$

Subject to $x_o - X\mu \geq 0$

$\eta y_o - Y\mu \leq 0$

$\mu \geq 0$

Equation-16:

$$DLP_o \min_{\theta,\lambda} \quad \theta$$

Subject to

$$\theta x_o \ - X\lambda \geq 0\text{--}$$

$$y_o - Y\lambda \leq 0$$

$$\lambda \geq 0$$

Equation-17:

$$\theta^* = \min_{\theta,\lambda s^- s^+} \theta - \varepsilon e s^+$$

Subject to

$$\theta x_o = \textstyle\sum_{j=1,\neq 0}^{n} \lambda_j \, x_j \ + s^-$$

$$y_o \sum_{j=1,\neq 0}^{n} \lambda_j \, y_j - s^+$$

Equation-18:

$$\delta_o^* = \min_{\psi,\ \lambda} \frac{1}{1 - 1/s \sum_{r=1}^{s} \psi r}$$

Subject to $\sum_{j=1,\neq o}^{n} x_{ij} \lambda_j \leq x_o (i = 1, \dots \dots .., m)$

$$\sum_{j=1,\neq o}^{n} y_{rj} \lambda_j + y_{ro} \psi_r \geq y_{ro} \, (r = 1, \dots \dots ., s)$$

$$\psi_r \geq 0 \; for \; all \; r \; and \; \lambda_j \geq 0 \; for \; all \; j$$

Executive Summary

In order to study the present structure and functioning of individual department, to calculate the relative efficiency of each department, the input-output slacks, the peer groups of the inefficient departments, projection of input mix/output mix that the department can reduce/ increase without affecting the current level of output, the study undertakes an empirical analysis of the efficiency evaluation of all the departments (27) of Sikkim University. The study has used two models of DEA such as CCR, BCC to compute the efficiency and rankings of each department (using five inputs and producing three outputs) under three different situations: (1) when all the departments are considered with all inputs and all outputs; (2) when two departments such as math and tour are merged with Phy and Geog using the same inputs and output; (3) five departments have been merged to see the changes in the rankings and efficiency scores of the departments. Lastly, Super efficiency model has been utilised (Radial, SBM output oriented and non-oriented model) to rank the fully efficient DMUs since all the fully efficient DMUs under CCR model are assigned the value 1.

As far as the scale of operation is concerned, 17 DMUs were fully efficient. Hence, they are operating under CRS and three DMUs (Eco, Soc and Comm.) are projected to operate under CRS.

However, one fully BCC efficient DMU, Phy is operating under DRS and DMUs are projected to be operating under DRS such as (IR, Psc, Bot, Chem., Eng and Geog). Hence, 17 DMUs are considered to be most Productive Scale and Size. These DMUs have the characteristics of radial expansion and contraction without any proportionate change in input output ratio.

In case of CCR model (1st case) the share of contribution of 2nd output (AM) is much higher to the improvement in efficiency followed by the 1st output (TRS). For Eco, Psc, Eng and Comm., production of 2nd output have largest share (more than 80 per cent) in the efficiency score.

While moving to the 2nd case, out of 25 DMUs, 15 DMU become fully efficient and 10 DMUs remain less efficient. The mean efficiency score is 0.911 with a SD of 0.13. PCM acted as the most frequently referred DMU (7 times) followed by Hind and edu (6 and 5 times respectively) for the inefficient DMUs. The fully efficient DMUs are (Masc, Mang, Hist, Edu, Law, Pcm, Psy, Antro, Nep, Hort, Micb, Hind, Geol, Phy and Chin) and the inefficient DMUs are (Bot, Eco, Comm., Soc, Chem., IR, Geog, Eng and Psc). The mean efficiency of the inefficient DMUs is 0.75 i.e., there is chance of 25 per cent improvement on an average of all inefficient DMUs.

Due to merging of tour with Geog, geog become fully efficient and similarly phy became fully efficient. Under BCC model, the mean efficiency score improved to 0.94 with a minimum score of 0.68. The number of fully efficient DMUs 17 and inefficient DMUs are 8. There is no change in positions of other DMUs. The only change under this situation is that merging made these two DMUs fully efficient without having any bad consequences for other DMUs.

The returns to scale indicate that 16 DMUs who are both CCR and BCC efficient are operating under CRS and comm is projected to be operating under CRS. One BCC efficient DMU (geog) is operating under DRS and other seven inefficient DMUs are projected to be operating under DRS. As realised from the observed input-output combination, some DMUs have very less number of outputs and inputs which will constrain the feasible region of operation. Hence, five DMUs (as discussed in the methodology) were allowed to merge with related DMUs (functional similarity). Out of all the outputs the NFD is dropped in this case. Under this situation the number of efficient DMUs reduced to seven and 15 DMUs could not achieve full efficiency. The mean efficiency (CCR) score is 0.818 which is less compared to earlier two cases. The fully efficient DMUs are (Edu, Psy, Antro, Hind, PCM, Zool). After merging geol with Chem, Math with Phy, Chin with Eng, Law with PSC and tour with Geog, except Phy no other DMUs could achieve full efficiency. The mean efficiency of inefficient DMUs is calculated to be 0.734 i.e., they can improve their performance at least by 27 per cent. Under the situation, Geog is ranked as the least performed DMU.

Under BCC model, the number of full efficient DMUs increased to 10 and 12 DMUs remained inefficient. The mean score is calculated to be 0.896 with a minimum score of 0.54. The most frequently chosen peer DMU is Hind (11 times) followed by PCM (7 times) and Psy (6 times). The fully BCC efficient DMUs are Mang, Edu, Psy, Antro, PCM, Hind, Phy, Chem., Zool, Micb) still Geog, Eng remained inefficient whereas, the rank of Geog improved to 18 and rank of eng reduced to 21. The least performed DMU is Comm. with a score of 0.545.

Out of the 10 fully efficient DMUs, seven are operating under CRS (PCM, Hind, Antro, PSY, Edu, Phy, Zool). The rest DMUs (Chem., Micb and Mang) are projected to operate under DRS. The three inefficient DMUs are projected to operate under DRS (Psc, Hort and Geog). The other nine DMUs are projected to be operating under DRS. The implication is that those DMUs operating under CRS can either expand or contract the output without changing the input ratio.

But those operating under DRS, suggests that DMUs are shortage of some of inputs and huge excess of the variable inputs. So expansion of the fixed inputs in comparison to variable inputs could change the scale of operation. The most interesting fact is that the no DMU is operating under IRs indicating the situation that no DMU has unutilised fixed inputs.

Further, the application of super efficiency model ranks the model fully efficient DMU. As per the three models, Chin, Pcm and Law ranked as the top ranked DMUs (with a slight change in position) and Hist, Mang and Micb remained at the lowest of the ranking of fully efficient DMU. It means these DMUs cant reduce the output if they are to remain efficient. Hence, the entire analysis suggests that Psy, PCM, Hind, Antro, Zool and Edu remained fully efficient in all the three situations. When Math and Tour are merged, it improved the efficiency of Phy and Geog to full efficiency without affecting other DMUs. But under the 3rd case, the merging has a bad impact even on the fully efficient DMUs. Except Phy, no other DMU in which other DMUs are merged could achieve full efficiency. It means size of operation does not allow the merging to be beneficial except Math and Tour.

Based on the results of efficiency analysis of all the departments of Sikkim University, the following suggestions have been proposed for the improvement of inefficient DMUs. As far as the inputs are considered, the area under the department has positive correlation with the number of permanent faculties. Therefore, both expansion of area and recruitment of permanent faculties are essentially required for departments who are inefficient and operating under diminishing returns to scale. Lack of permanent faculties not only affects the teaching quality but also reduce the output on research activities. Hiring of ad hoc faculties only enhances the current expenditure without adding anything to the enhancement of efficiency. Therefore, huge investment on building, permanent infrastructure (class-rooms, laboratory, faculty rooms, departmental library, central library equipped with textbooks, referred books, back volumes of journals, current journals, data bases, computer lab with all modern facilities, rooms for M.Phil and PhD students. Since, the university does not have permanent campus; the current expenditure has become huge irrespective of the size of the operation (number of students admitted into the course, number of courses launched and number of teachers engaged). The variable cost for maintenance remains almost same and it goes on increasing as the size is increasing above a certain level. Therefore, total expenditure of the small departments is not so small compared to the large departments. Hence, centralised structure for the university is an urgent need. From the data, it is clear that Social Sciences consisting of seven departments has no professor (2014-15) and only four associate professors. On an average, the school of Social Sciences has only three faculties. The situation is worse in school of languages, Human Science and Professional Studies. Therefore, urgent attention must be given towards; recruitment of faculties without considering the fact those financial constraints dominates over the issue. As per the data, the girls' students in almost all the departments perform better than the boys in their respective courses. Therefore, more attention should be given for the improvement of the performances of boys in their courses. Since, the girls enrolment in Science subjects are less, efforts must initiated to make the science course attractive for the girls student. Further, the admission procedure for the girls' students in the science stream should be relaxed to an allowable limit for better enrolment of girls' students. Counseling of students and parents at the UG and PG level must be made to persuade the students into these streams. As in some of the departments, the average marks of the students is less than or equal to 50 per cent, the nature of the subject calls for strict attendance of the students. Failing of strict attendance norms develop a casual behaviour on attending classes regularly. This might be one of the reasons for low performance of the male students. Second, the examination system should enforce prohibition of the students failing the attendance of the required percentage. Compulsory crash courses should be given in technical subjects (Eco, Math, Phy, Chem) to the weak students who are unable to cope of with the course in the first semester itself. The result suggests that the improvement of inefficient departments in the first case (CCR and BCC model) could be achieved by focusing more on TRS and AM. The faculties must allocate qualitative time for teaching the courses. Strict enforcement of good quality teaching with high standard must be enforced seriously to improve the standard of teaching. The merging of Math and Tour with Phy and Geog improves the position of the Phy and Geog efficiency without adversely affecting the rankings and scores of other departments. Therefore, merging of these two departments is strongly recommended to have overall improvement in the efficiency. Further merger other departments such as Geol with Chem, Math with Phy, Chin with Eng, Law with PSC and Tour with Geog do not seem to be favourable for overall improvement of the departments. Rather, the number of departments operating under full efficiency reduced to seven and the number of inefficient departments increased to 15. Therefore, merger at large scale of the above departments is not suggested as the differences in the size of operation do not allow being beneficial. In all the cases, Psy, PCM, Hind, Antro, Zool and Edu remained peers for all other inefficient departments. These departments are considered as the most productive in scale and size. These departments can be considered as role models for others at the existing input-output structure. On the basis of super efficiency ranking, Chin, PCM and Law remained as the top super efficient department with top ranks in all three cases and Hist, Mang and Micb remained as the lowest ranked fully efficient departments. Since no department under no case is operating under increasing returns to scale, the stage of operation of each department is not at primary level. As majority of departments are projected to be operating under DRS, policy should be focused on expansion of fixed assets as mentioned above.

Chapter -1

Introduction

1.1. Introduction

The memorable address that Theodore Schultz made to the American Economic Association in December, 1960, became a significant academic debate of research within the domain of economics profession that education can be regarded as an investment in '*Human Capital*'. The human, as invests in capital, decides to invest in their own education. The study of economics of education centrally focused on the demand for education. Psacharopoulos and Patrinos (2004) argued that the role of education is to play in raising individual's productivity.

Since 1970s, economists have also thought of another dimension that intends to examine the interrelationship between human education and earnings. These models essentially use 'signaling and screening' models. Such models focus on the role played by educational credentials as individuals' innate ability and productivity. Firms that are unable to reward productive-individuals could use education as a signal of individual productivity. Whatever may be the merits of the human capital, the signaling and the screening models in the sphere of formal education, one would essentially expect vocational training programmes to contribute directly to the productivity of the trainee (Dolton, 1985).

In the recent advancement of educational research outcome, strong evidence has been emerged in the last decade of the impact that education can have on economic growth. The fast growth in many South and East Asian economies along with extensive growth of educational institutions and educational provisions has given ample evidence that the key role education can play in augmenting and stimulating economic development (Stevens and Weale, 2004).

1.2. Human Capital and Rates of Return

The seeds of theoretical linkage between education and productivity originated in the writings of the classical economists but remained unrecognised or dormant till the remarkable speech made by T.W. Schultz that marked the beginning of the modern '*Human Capital*' school. The most historical remark among the classicals is Adam Smith's (1776) classic statement that compared the educated man to a most expensive machine. Alfred Marshall (1890), referred to industrial training as a national investment in his *Principles of Economics*. Soon after Russian Revolution, a Soviet economist made estimates of the benefits of the nation from investment in universal primary and secondary education (Strumlin, 1924). Walsh (1935) estimated the returns to the formal schooling and graduate students in USA. Friedman and Kuznet (1946) estimated the income of doctors and dentists.

1.3. Signalling and Screening

Two contrasting views on the relationship between education and earnings have been emerged in recent years. One, the theory of '*Human Capital*' holds that education directly augments individual productivity and therefore, earnings (Schultz, 1961; Mincer, 1974; Becker, 1975). Hence, forgoing current income and acquiring more and more education can improve the quality of their labour services in such a way as to raise their future market value. The alternative view- the '*Sorting Hypothesis*' proved that education also signals and screens intrinsic productivity (Spence, 1973; Arrow, 1973; Stiglitz, 1975). Higher levels of education are linked to higher earning not because they increase productivity but because they certify that the worker is understandably a good input for smart work. The reasons behind as argued are: they remain less absent; less propensities to quit the job; less likely to smoke; to drink or to use illicit drugs. Since these attributes are less visible during hiring, the firms take levels of education as proxy for this.

1.4. Education and Economic Growth

Two important arguments made to find the link between education and economic growth are: one, it is intuitively possible that living standards have risen so much over the last millennium and in particular since 1800 century because of education. Progress of the type realised in Europe was not observed in the comparatively illiterate society that has gradually merged into the world economy over the last two hundred years. Secondly, at a more concrete level, a wide range of econometric studies indicates that the incomes individual can earn depend upon their level of education.

As a link between education and economic performance in various countries with regard to primary school enrolment provided by Maddison (1991) indicated that the high levels of GDP per capita are associated with high levels of enrolment. The further econometric analysis suggested that one per cent increase in the enrolment raises GDP by 0.35 per cent. Because education delivers economic benefit to individuals, it should be expected that it also benefits the group of individuals. A classic study by Miner (1974) found that for white males not working on firms, an extra year of education raised the earnings of an individual by about seven per cent. However, earnings appeared to be an increasing linear and decreasing quadratic function of years of work. As per the survey of Psacharopoulos (1994) over 78 countries show returns to primary education ranging from 42 per cent per annum in Botswana to only 3.3 per cent per annum in former Yugoslavia and two per cent in Yemen. The largest return was 47.6 per cent in Zimbabwe. The range of tertiary education was somewhat narrower between -4.3 per cent in Zimbabwe and 24 per cent per annum in Yemen.

1.5. Indirect Benefits of Education

1.5.1. Social and External Benefits of Education

In addition to the direct benefits that education levels of a person provides, there are external benefits from education of each individual. These include education's impact on economic development goals that are important part of quality goals that are important part of life and also it benefits the future generation. There have been ample of research works relevant to education externalities. These include Haveman and Wolfe, (1984) and MacMohan (1987). The work of Wolfe and Haveman (2001) focuses primarily on non-market private returns.

The non-market effects of education are presented in Table-1 just given below.

Table 1.1: Non-Market Effects of Education

Private Benefits	Social Benefits
Private monetary benefits	Externality benefits to GDP/Capita
Private non-market benefits	Externality benefits, non market
Pure Public good externalities	Pure public good externalities

Source: Walter. W Mcmohan. The Social and External Benefits of Education (p. 24) in Geriant Johnes and Jill Johnes (2004) International Handbook of Economics of Education.

1.6. Rankings and Reshaping of Higher Education: The Battle for World Class Excellence

There is a growing consciousness with the university ranking around the world. Started as an academic exercise in the early twentieth century, it became a 'commercial' information service for the students in 1980's resulting into a situation of reputation race with geographical implication. This ranking consciousness became more serious in response to globalisation and the persuit of new knowledge as the basis of economic growth, and the drive for increased public accountability and transparency. Ranking has become the "Battle for Excellence" and determines the status of the individual institutions and gauge its global competitiveness. In this process, rankings of the universities are transforming and reshaping higher education system.

The transformation of higher education environment over the last few decades has been well documented (CERI, 2009; Marginson and Van der Wende, 2007; Altbach *et. al.*, 2010). Out of several perspectives, the four important drivers of the speed and depth of revolution impacting on higher education and the extents of changes required are:

- The shift of focus from increasing productivity and efficiency to higher valued goods through talent. Today almost 80 per cent of a company's value comes from soft knowledge- unique knowledge of services, markets, relationship reputation and brand (Hutton, 2006).

  Research shows that productivity growth in USA has been generated largely by advances of technology driven by a number of innovations (Chellaraj *et. al.*, 2005). In turn, this has positioned higher education a provider of human capital through education and training, a source of new knowledge. Government and policy-makers have put their endeavour to steer and restructure higher education in ways which, while supporting autonomy, use performance-based funding and, in many cases institutional contracts to ensure higher education meets its social and economic objectives.

- The second factor is when countries are dependent on talent, many are under demographic pressure. Knowing that people with higher education are more likely to migrate the government, as a counter-measure, are seeking better alignment between higher education, innovation and immigration policies to guarantee access to global talent pool.

- Third, the higher education has been transformed from being considered a social expenditure to being an essential component of productive economy. There is increasing emphasis on value-for-money, productivity and efficiency, and ensuring investor confidence, often referred to as new public management (Deem, 2001) or 'modernisation' agenda (Europa, 2006). The extent of changes, though vary across nations, includes restructuring academic programmes to make them more compatible, competitive and attractive. More emphasis on research targets and outputs which are measurable and supported by competitively earned funding, merging departments to promote efficiency (Rhodes, 2004; Haze,l Korn and Mounihan, 2010).
- Finally, because education and graduate outcomes and life styles are strongly correlated with higher qualifications and career opportunity, students and their parents have become savvy consumers (Santiago *et. al.,* 2008). The development of high technology have major consequences for higher education and have been responsible for transforming it into a key instrument of economic development and it has transformed Higher Education Institutions (HEI) into private market and performance driven competing university-as-firms (Morginson, 2010). This has involved application of business principles and management processes, with a strong emphasis on accountability, transparency and performances. Because higher education plays a fundamental role in creating competitive advantage in a market environment, performance matters. Therefore, the objectives of HEI settles into two related objectives: (i) maximising the capacity and performance within the global landscape, and (ii) optimising benefits of the linkages of national and local settings (Van der Wende, 2009).

1.7. The Importance of Measuring Productivity in Higher Education

The famous sayings of William Bruce Cameron- "Not everything that counts can be counted and not everything that can be counted counts" is applicable to higher education.

Beyond the production of good citizens, academic institutions also perform much of the nation's research and development. Academic institutions performed 55 per cent of basic research and 31 per cent of the total research in United States (National Science Board, 2010). Recent research (Carnevale, Smith and Strohl, 2010) indicate that the expanding industries rely on workers with higher educational credentials. The demand for higher education made the HEI to concern about improving their performances. In this context, interest on the performance on higher education has become a burning issue for the academicians and policy-makers. In higher education, productivity improvement is seen as the most promising strategy for containing costs in the continuing effort to keep higher education affordable. Hence, concepts such as productivity and efficiency and accountability are central to the sustainability, cost and quality of higher education.

1.8. Education Outcome Provision

"Equality of Educational Opportunity" for the US Department of Education widely known as Coleman Report (1966) can be conceived as the starting point for viewing education as a productive process. It provided the evidence that the socioeconomic factors of the students are the most important factor determining the educational outcome of the pupil. Parental background and student characteristics have a bigger effect in addition to the school resources. In this context, Hanushek (1979, 1986) provides a useful foundation to analyse education as a production process where outcomes are functions of school-inputs and socio-economic variables. The similar studies such as Bridge, Judd and Moock (1979),

Cohn and Jeske (1990) provide insights of the education production process.

In another aspect Leibenstein (1966), Nisknen (1971, 1975), Mighe and Belanger (1974) provided useful political framework for the existence of efficiency of schools. Instead of profit maximising or cost minimising firms bureaucrats are inclined to either maximise their budgets or excess spending which could lead to inefficiency.

1.8.1 Educational Production and Efficiency

In case of education, the prices of inputs (discretionary) are readily available, the prices of the outcome are neither well defined nor readily available or observed. Data Envelopment Analysis (DEA) is the term coined in the operation research literature by Charnes, Cooper and Rhodes (CCR-1978) to measure the technical efficiency of a given observed Decision Making Unit (DMU) assuming CRS production technology for multi-input and multi-output correspondence. Further, Banker, Charnes and Cooper (1984) extended it to analyse decomposition of technical and scale efficiency using VRS (Variable Returns to Scale) technology. The most significant literature on educational production using DEA is Banker and Morey (1986) which allowed Non-Discretionary inputs. Alternative models allowing socio-economic variables are (Ray, 1988, 1991: McCarty and Yaisawarng, 1993). Fare and Grosskopf and Weber (1989) measured efficiency of Missouri schools and utilised discretionary inputs and standardised tests.

Ruggeiro, Duncombe and Miner (1985) measured the inefficiency of New York school districts and sought to explain the causes from the bureaucratic model. Ruggeiro (1998) provided a cost framework whereby the cost efficiency of school districts could be measured. He further used DEA to show the estimate of the cost of producing a given education (Ruggeiro, 2001).

DEA has also been extended to measure public sector productivity with applications to education. Ouellette and Vierstraete (2010), Johnson and Ruggeiro (2011), Brennan, Haelermans and Ruggeiro (2013), Essid and Onellette and Vigeant (2014) provided a Malmquist decomposition of productivity in the presence of fixed factors of production. Essid et. al., (2014) analyses Tunisian schools in the context of using quasi-fixed factors. Efficiency of Dutch schools was studied by Haelermans, De Witte and Blank (2012) and Haelerman and Ruggeiro (2013).

1.9. Setting of the Problem

Accountability, value for money, cost-effectiveness, transparency and moreover, measurement of organisational efficiency is recognised as an integral part of implementation, monitoring and constant evaluation irrespective of the nature of the organisation whether profitable or non-profitable. Higher education sector of many countries especially the universities obtain some of their public funds making it essential in the interest of accountability, to measure the efficiency of institutions which comprise these sectors. Over the past few years, India's Higher Education sector has witnessed tremendous growth. Today the country has the largest education system in the world in terms of the number of institutions, second in terms of enrolment. Improving the efficiency of educational systems is a growing concern of educational planners and academicians in the recent years. The key concern for India is the creation of an employable workforce to harness its demographic dividend to maximum extent. Improving ***Skill, Speed and Scale*** at micro-unit level in the higher educational institutions especially in the universities of National character must be focused to achieve the development agenda of ***Sabkaa Saath Sabkaa Bikaash.***

1.9.1. Statement of the Problem

Since efficiency lies at the forefront of policy debates

around restructuring of the educational institutions' functioning, study of efficiency of the university at departmental level is a necessity. Using the inputs and outputs of each individual departments of the Sikkim University, the project proposes to empirically investigate the basic structure and functioning of each department, determining the efficient and inefficient performer, identifying the input and output slacks of each department, identifying the role model for the inefficient departments, determining the possibilities of improvement and to determine the super efficient department among all the efficient departments. The study has future relevance in terms of measuring and decomposing the total productivity over the periods of time.

1.10. Review of the Literature

Critical review of literature focuses on the issue of measurement of efficiency of educational institutions, alternative statistical and mathematical methods used and the empirical studies on educational institutions.

1.10.1. Issues in Measuring Efficiency of Educational Institutions

The most common conceptual frameworks used in the analysis of economics of education is seen in the form of production function by considering educational institutions analogous to a typical firm transforming inputs into output through a production process. Teaching and learning environments are generally considered as inputs for the education production and outputs are generally considered as students score as well as teachers' performance in the research outcome. Despite much of empirical research there is no strong empirical evidence exists to support the contention that traditional educational inputs have the expected positive influence on the educational outcomes (Pritchet and Filmer, 1999). The reasons of this failure are: validity of the educational production function framework itself; ineffective measurable outcome as innate ability, socio-economic background may dominate educational production process (Deller and Rudnicki, 1993); lack of positive relationship between educational outcome and educational expenditure (Mayston, 1996) and the assumption of efficiency i.e. all the educational institutions are capable of transforming the inputs and outputs at the same rate and this is not true in reality (Hanushek, 1986). Assuming existence of inefficiency among the educational institutions, various techniques have been employed to identify efficient educational institutions and compare them with inefficient institutions. The methods used to resolve the problem of efficiency of these institutions starts from the use of Ordinary Least Square Method (OLS) to the recent studies use frontier methods such as Data Envelopment or Stochastic Frontier Analysis (SFA) (Johnes, 2006).

1.10.2. Theoretical Foundations of Efficiency Measurement

The measurement of efficiency begins with Farrell (1957) who defined efficiency for multiple inputs. He suggested that the use of either (a) non-parametric piecewise linear convex isoquant constructed such that no observed point should lie to the left or below it or (b) parametric function such as Cobb-Douglas form fitted to the data such that no point should lie to the left or below it. The parametric approach specifies the production function and the deviation from the technology are composed of two parts: *statistical noise* and the other is *inefficiency*. The inefficiencies follow an asymmetric half normal distribution and random errors are normally distributed and it captures all uncontrollable factors in the production. This specification led to the development of Stochastic Frontier Approach (SFA). The inefficiency could be measured by a variety of statistical techniques including corrected OLS, modified OLS and Maximum Likelihood Estimation (MLE). However, this method is beset by the problem of misspecification of the functional form and inappropriate when multiple outputs are produced using multiple inputs especially in case of educational institutions. The other mathematical programming approach is commonly known as the Data Envelopment Analysis (DEA). It calculates the efficiency of a given organisation relative to the performance of other organisation producing the same good or service rather than against an idealised standard performance. Worthington (2001) presents the detailed review of the studies using SFA and DEA. Despite some limitations of DEA (Smith and Mayston, 1987), there are substantial numbers of benefits implicit in the techniques such as: freedom on specification of inputs and output; insight into the inefficiency calculation and interpretation of slack variables for those who are in the frontier as well as not in the frontier. The theoretical and empirical considerations explain the dominance of DEA in education efficiency measurement studies (Worthington, 2001). The details of Data Envelopment Analysis (DEA) is presented in Chapter 2.

Sengupta and Sfer (1986), analysed the existence of the economies of scale in taking the sample of 25 Californian school and found that frontier techniques to be more stable than the non-frontier techniques. Studies made on universities include (Athanassopoulos and Shale, 1997), on universities departments (Sinuany-Stern *et. al.*, 1994; Beasley 1990, 1995 and Madden *et. al.,* 1997). There is generally greater agreement among educational efficiency studies regarding the specification of inputs. Students test score is the most preferred educational outcome in case of school level. In case of university departments teaching research and research grants are the inputs and outputs are measured in categories of published works and referred journal articles (Johnes and Johns, 1993, 1995; Beasley, 1995 and Madden *et. al.,* 1997). As per the survey by Worthington (2001) on studies on efficiency of educational institutions, the major factors of determining the level of inefficiencies of the organisation are: parental socio-economic background, proportion of minority students, proportion of students from rich family background, parental education teachers' experience.

1.11. Objectives of the Study

1. To study the present structure and functioning of each department.
2. To calculate the relative efficiency scores of each department producing multi-output using multi-inputs and thereby estimating the input excesses and output shortfalls of the inefficient departments.
3. To project the role models (peer group) of each inefficient department and to determine the benchmark level of input and output-mix for an inefficient performer.
4. To make a projection on the targeted input-mix and/ or the output-mix that an inefficient department can reduce and /or increase without negatively affecting the current level of output-mix produced and/ or input-mix used.
5. To estimate the ranks of the fully efficient departments and to project the input expansion despite its position in the frontier.
6. To study the exogenous factors of inefficiency, and
7. To suggest measures to be taken to bring the inefficient departments onto the frontier.

1.12. Methodology

1.12.1. Nature, Type and Sources of Data

In order to estimate the efficiency of individual departments of Sikkim University as proposed in the proposal, the data on inputs and outputs of each department have been collected. The input output data are of the following nature.

The outputs are : (1) teaching and Research Score (TRS); (2) Average Marks Scored (AM), and (3) No. of First Divisions (NFD). As far as TRS is concerned, data on no. of papers (both national and international) conferences attended, paper presented in the conferences, research projects carried out (both major and minor) special lecture delivered, M.Phil and PhD students registered, conferences organised, refresher and Orientation courses attended by the faculties have been collected. The scores for each item have been computed as per the UGC guidelines. The total score in numbers have been computed for each department individually.

The second output is the Average Marks (AM) of the students of a department. The aggregate scores an individual student obtained in the PG course for the year 2015 pass out students have been collected. The average marks for a particular department has been computed by dividing the total marks of all the students in a department divided by the total number of students passed the course. While considering the marks, only those departments who have PG courses are taken into considerations. Therefore, in this criteria, Department of Computer Application and Music are excluded. (Presently, department of Computer Application is having both UG and PG course).

The third output considered in the analysis is the no of first division students (60 per cent and above). While computing the aggregate marks, the score of 60 per cent and above has been considered as first division; the score above 50 per cent and below 60 per cent is considered as second divisions and the pass students with less than 50 per cent are considered as third divisions.

There are five inputs considered for the DEA analysis. These are: (1) The total area utilised by a department (in square feet), (2) no. of Permanent faculties (assistant, associate and professors taken together); (3) total expenditure incurred on each department; (4) no. of male first division students and (5) no. of female first division students. Since the university does not have the permanent campus till date, hired buildings are taken on rent basis to run the activities. Therefore, the area under the department has been considered. This not only reflects the student class room ratio but also the gives an impression of the minimum requirement of are for smooth functioning of a department. Secondly, while considering the no. of permanent faculties, the issue of the ad hoc teaching faculties are ignored, as these faculties only take teaching activity relation and do not contribute anything on the research activities. Since they are paid and the payment is included in the total expenditure, it is thought to be appropriate to exclude these faculties from being considered.

As far as the types of data are concerned, the information on all these inputs and outputs has been collected from the various issues of the Annual Reports of the Sikkim University. The information is collected for all the existing 29 departments but the analysis is done for only 27 departments as two departments are not having PG courses in the year under consideration of this study. The official information on marks no. of students passed, the total marks obtained, gender-wise marks are obtained from the Office of Controller of Examination, Sikkim University. The Financial-related information have been collected from the Office of Finance officer, the information related to the area possessed by each department have been collected from the Office of Registrar, the Sikkim University.

As per the objectives mentioned above, the study uses Data Envelopment Analysis (DEA technique) to estimate the department-wise efficiency scores and the ranking of the departments. The reason behind the comparative superiority of this method over other alternatives has been explained in Chapter 2 in detailed manner.

1.13. Chapterisation

The entire report has been divided into four main chapters. Chapter One briefly explains the importance of higher education to economic growth and the importance of ranking of universities and thereby the necessity of measuring the efficiency of the departments functioning in the university. This chapter after giving a brief survey of the literature on measuring efficiency of educational institutions outlines the objectives of the study, the type of sources and the nature of the data. The first chapter ends with small hints about the methods of analysis employed in the study.

Hence, the Second Chapter discusses about the theoretical background of Efficiency evaluation. The chapter deals with the meaning of efficiency, types of efficiency and the methods available to measure the efficiency level. The last section brings out the CCR and BCC model of DEA and the concept of Super Efficiency to rank the fully efficient units that could not be assigned distinct number other than 1.

Chapter - 2

Theoretical Background of Efficiency Evaluation

2.1. Concept of Efficiency

The measurement of how well educational institutions perform has been the subject of increased attention in recent years. Variables linked to measure different aspects of schools and universities are often take the form of ratios which represent efficiency in producing outputs or efficiency in using resources. This simple performance measures aims at informing the consumers to take appropriate choice and resource allocation.

The dangers involved with these so called indicators are: the institutions of particular interest (schools and universities) operate under different conditions and different environments which cannot be accounted by simple ratios; the institutions of education produce an array of outputs from a range of inputs. So ratio of one output to one input cannot capture the complete performance of the organisations.

The consequence is the direction of academic research towards developing a number of techniques and application have been also made to measure the true efficiency of organisations. Statistical techniques have been developed from simple Ordinary Least Squares Methods (OLS) to more developed Stochastic Frontier Analysis (SFA) and simple ratios of one output to one input have been replaced by composite ratios of efficiency developed by linear programming.

2.2. Definition Of Efficiency

The starting point of any discussion on the concept must begin with Farrell (1957) who defines three types of efficiency which will be explained below with the help of Figure 2.1.

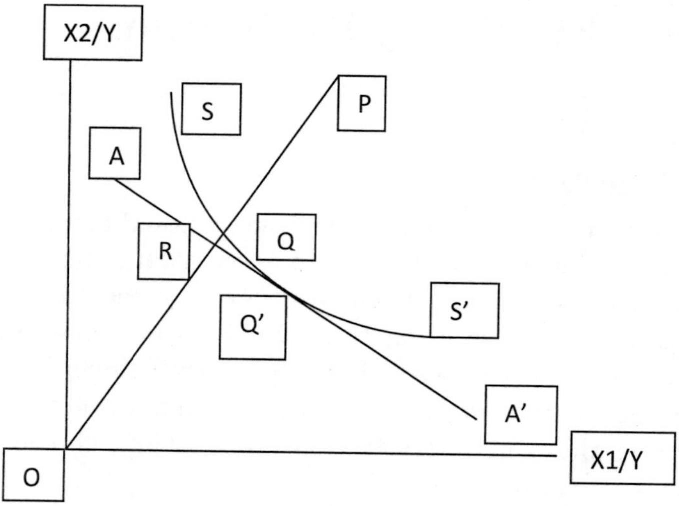

Fig. 2.1: Technical, Allocative and Economic Efficiency

Consider a firm which uses inputs X1 and X2 to produce a given level of output Y. The point is denoted by P. The isoquant SS' is the locus of all the technologically possible combinations of X1 and X2 producing a given level of output. The efficient firm will try to utilise any combinations on the isoquant. The technology that transforms the inputs into output used is assumed to be characterised by Constant Returns to Scale (CRS).

The Technical Efficiency (TE) of the firm producing at point P in the XY space is defined as the proportion of inputs used by the firm which is actually necessary to produce the output observed at point P is TE= OQ/OP (the minimum amount of input required/ The actual input used). Hence,

1-TE could be defined as the measure of technical inefficiency. This measure suggests the proportion by which the firms input could be reduced (without changing the input ratio) while keeping the level of output constant (Worthington, 2001).

However, this measure does not take into account the input prices to which the firm is very sensitive. Hence, further measure of efficiency can be defined by introducing the price information by means a line AA' that shows the price ratio of the two inputs. The point Q', the tangency point of the isoquant and price line shows both technical efficiency (TE) and allocative efficiency (AE) (or Price efficiency). This shows the optimal input used with minimum cost. The minimum cost of inputs (optimal inputs) that do not change the ratio of inputs used at P is same as at R., hence, the measure of Allocative Efficiency (AE) is AE= (OR/OQ). Point Q and Q' are technically efficient but the cost of production at Q' are fraction of OR/OQ of the costs at Q. The cost that can be reduced to produce the same output is PQ. Finally, the overall (Economic Efficiency/ Total Economic Efficiency) (OE) of the firm is defined as OE = OR/OP. This OE is the product of TE and AE i.e., (OQ/OP) (OR/OQ) = OR/OP=OE.

The quantity 1- OE is therefore, the measure of inefficiency. The distance RP represents the reduction in the costs of production that could be attained by switching its production point from P to cost minimising point Q'. This above approach conceived by Farrell (1957) is basically input oriented that seeks to answer the question: by how much can the firm reduce proportionally without changing the quality of output reduced?

In a parallel way one can define the *Output-Oriented* approach to the measure of above three concepts of efficiency. The Figure-2.2 shows the TE, AE and OE in *Output Oriented* framework.

In this context, the firm produces two outputs using a given quantity of input X. In the context of education, the

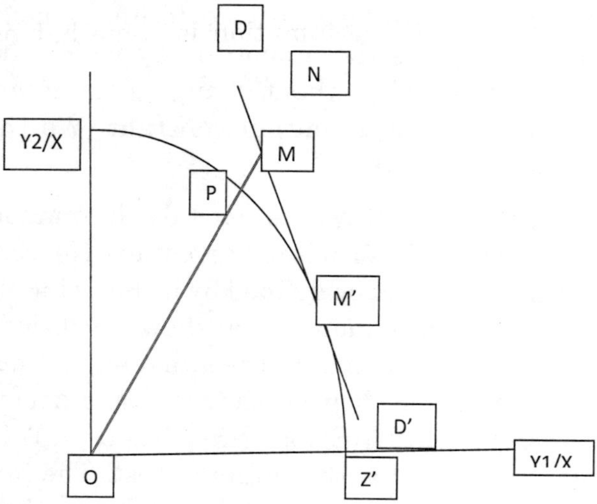

Fig. 2.2: Measuring TE, AE and OE in an output Oriented framework.

firm is the educational institution (may be school, college or university) and it might be producing output of teaching (Y1) and Research (Y2) from one input staff (X). The production possibility frontier (PPF) shows the technically efficient combinations of output. The TE of the firm is TE = OP/OM. In this case, 1-TE which, is measure of inefficiency measures the proportion by which the firm can increase the output without increasing the level of input at the observed production point P. Allocative efficiency (AE) is defined as AE = OM/ON. By introducing the *iso-revenue* line DD', the firm chooses that output combination which maximises revenue. The point both M and M' are TE but point M' is both TE and AE. But the revenue from the production at N is the fraction OM/ON of the revenue at M' and the increase in the revenue which the firm could achieve by producing the correct output proportion of the Distance MN. The overall Efficiency (OE) is OE = O/ON.

1-OE is a measure of inefficiency and the distance is the amount by which the firm could increase its revenue by moving from P to M'. The efficiency score obtained under both orientation under CRS assumption is same but not with variable returns to scale (VRS) scenario.

2.3. Techniques for Measuring Efficiency

The survey of literature gives evidence of the use of two basic approaches: *Statistical* (econometric) approach and *Programming approach* (Non-Statistical). The former approach assumes a definite probability distribution for the efficiency of the firm (Forsund *et. al.,* 1980). Secondly, this approach assumes a particular functional form for the underlaying production function (example *Cobb Douglas, Constant Elasticity and Translog)* (Sengupta, 1999). The mis-specifications of the errors (either specifying the production function or inefficiency distribution) are incorporated in the efficiency measure (Lovell, 1993). However, this approach is failed to be used in case of multiproduct firm.

The *programming/non-statistical* approach, on the other hand, makes no assumption with regard to the distribution of inefficiencies. The input and output data, using linear programming, computes the *convex hull* to represent the efficiency frontier, (Sengupta, 1999). Hence, this method avoids the problem of mis-specification of functional form and distribution of inefficiencies. Further, this method allows use of multiple input-output production process.

The final distinction between these alternative methods is that they can be either stochastic or deterministic (Schmidt, 1985; Lovell, 1993). The SFA is based on the premise that any deviations from the production function are due to some composite error term: inefficiency term and statistical noise (Lovell, 1993; Ondrich and Ruggeiro, 2001). The model assumes specific distribution for each term.

Deterministic approach, on the other hand, assumes that any deviation from production frontier is due to inefficiency only. Any errors in the measurement are assumed to be incorporated in the measurement of efficiency. In short, the efficiency measurement can fall into statistical (deterministic or stochastic) and mathematical or *non-parametric.*

2.3.1. Statistical Approach

2.3.1.1. Deterministic Approach

Suppose the producer (firm/DMU) i transforms input (x) into output (y). The production function is specified as

$$Ln(y_i) = \ln[f(x_{i1, \dots \dots \dots}, x_{im})] - u_i$$

$$= \alpha_0 + \sum_{j=1}^{m} \alpha_j \, lnx_{ij} - u_i \dots \dots \dots \dots \dots \dots \dots \dots \dots \dots \dots (1)$$

The residual$-u_i$ where, $u_i \geq 0$ and it represents the efficiency of the producer. The TE of the firm is the ratio of actual output of the producer is to maximising possible output which it could produce as given by the frontier equation -1.

The TE is

$$\frac{y_i}{f(x_{i1,} \qquad x_{im}} = e^{-u} \dots \dots \dots \dots \dots \dots \dots \dots \dots \dots \dots \dots \dots (2)$$

Under the assumption of (Cobb Douglas technology (C-D), the parameters of the function are estimated using simple OLS method. The intercept is shifted until all residuals are non-positive. The alternative approach assumes an appropriate distribution for *(half-normal, exponential and Gamma)*. This approach is referred to as the *Corrected OLS* or Modifies OLS (Forsund *et.al.,* 1980; Lovell, 1993). Maximum Likelihood Method (MLE) can also be used as an alternative OLS to estimate simultaneously the assumed distribution of and the parameters of the function specified in equation -2. However, this method suffers from the defects that the methods are unsuitable for application where multi-inputs and outputs are used.

2.3.1.2. Stochastic Approach

In order to permit stochastic residuals in the methodology the equation 1 is modified in the following form (equation -3)

$$Ln(y_i) = \ln[f(x_{i1,} \dots \dots \dots \dots, x_{im})] + \varepsilon_i$$

Where the equation (2) becomes

$$Ln(y_i) = \ln[f(x_{i1,} \dots \dots \dots \dots, x_{im})] + \varepsilon_i$$

$$= \alpha_0 + \sum_{j=1}^{m} \alpha_j \, lnx_{ij} + \varepsilon_i \dots \dots \dots \dots \dots \dots \dots \dots \dots \dots \dots (3)$$

Where, $v_i \sim N(0, \sigma_v^2) and \; u_i \; and \; v_i$ are statistically independent $u_i \geq 0$ and (Aigner *et. al.*, 1977). The residualε_i is composed of two terms: one is the random error (v_i) attributed to the random fluctuation beyond the control of the firm and the second component(u_i) is attributed to technical inefficiency and its distribution can be *exponential or half-normal.* The parameters can be estimated using MOLS or MLE method. This method is known as Stochastic Frontier Analysis (SFA).

If u_i is assumed to be *half-normal* the log likelihood function is given by

$$\ln L = -n \ln \sigma - \frac{n}{2} ln \frac{2}{\pi} - \frac{1}{2} \sum_i \ln \phi \left(\frac{-\varepsilon_i \lambda}{\sigma} \right) \dots \dots \dots \dots \dots \dots \dots (4)$$

Where, $\sigma^2 = \sigma_u^2 + \sigma_v^2$ and $\lambda = \sigma_u / \sigma_v$ and ϕ is the *cumulative distribution function* of the standard normal function. Assuming the normality, u_i , the mean technical inefficiency is $\sigma_u \sqrt{2/\pi}$ and can be computed using σ_u . Further firm-specific technical efficiency (TE) can be computed by the technique developed by (Jondrow *et. al.*, 1982).

The Point estimate of u_i is then given by the mean of the conditional distribution

$$E(u_i|\varepsilon_i) = \frac{\sigma_u \sigma_v}{\sigma} [\frac{\Phi(\varepsilon_i \lambda/_{\sigma})}{1 - \Phi(\varepsilon_i \lambda/_{\sigma})} - \frac{\varepsilon_i \lambda}{\sigma} \quad \text{......}(5)$$

Despite its appealing mathematical property and grounding in economic theory, some critics have supported that the confidence interval of the inefficiency estimates might be large.

2.4. Non-Parametric (Deterministic) Approach

The most popular non-parametric approach used for measuring technical efficiency is known as Data Envelopment Analysis (DEA) attributed to Charnes, Cooper and Rhodes (1978) following the work of Dantzig (1951) and Farrell (1957).

2.4.1. CCR Model of DEA Method

The importance of specifying the DEA method arises owing to the fact that the entire project objective is to quantify the efficiency measures of the department of the university. Hence, interpretation of the result requires an understanding of the methodology on which the entire technique is based on.

Data Envelopment Analysis (DEA) was ascribed to this name because of the way it 'envelops' the observations in order to identify 'frontier' that is used to evaluate units of observations presenting the performances of all the entities that are to be evaluated uses DEA have been extended to a wider variety of entities including schools, hospitals, business organisations, military units, police forces, countries regions etc. The term Decision Making Unit (DMU) is used to describe such entities that are evaluated as a part of the whole that uses similar inputs to produce similar output. For, each DMU a virtual input and output is formed by unknown weights v_i and u_i respectively. Then the linear programming approach is used to maximise the ratio of weighted outputs (virtual output) to weighted inputs (virtual input).

Suppose there are n DMUs: DMU_1, DMU_2 and ...... DMU_n. The common inputs and outputs for each DMU (J=1, 2,..........,n) m inputs and s outputs. Since the ratio of virtual weight differs from DMU to DMU, the ratio to be maximized for DMU_0 is $\frac{virtual\ output}{virtual\ input}$

$$\frac{u_1 y_{10} + u_2 y_{20} +, \ldots\ldots + u_{sy} y_{s0}}{v_1 x_{10} + v_2 x_{20} +, \ldots\ldots + v_m x_{m0}} \ldots\ldots\ldots\ldots (6)$$

The CCR model (Charnes, Cooper and Rhodes, 1978) is specified as

$$(FP_o) \qquad \underset{v,u}{Max} \quad \theta = \frac{u_1 y_{10} + u_2 y_{20} +, \ldots\ldots + u_{sy} y_{s0}}{v_1 x_{10} + v_2 x_{20} +, \ldots\ldots + v_m x_{m0}} \ldots\ldots\ldots (7)$$

subject to

$$\frac{u_1 y_{1j} +, \ldots\ldots u_s y_{sj}}{v_1 x_{1j} + \cdots \ldots\ldots v_m x_{mj}} \leq 1 \ (j = 1,2, \ldots n) \ \ldots \ldots \ldots (8)$$

$$v_1, v_2\ v_3, \ldots \ldots \ldots \ldots v_n \geq 0$$

$$u_1, u_2, \ u_3, \ldots\ldots, u_s \geq 0$$

Due to the first constraints the optimal value θ^* cannot be more than 1. The LP formation from Fractional programming can be written as

$$(LP_o) \qquad \underset{\mu,v}{Max} \quad \theta = \mu_1 y_{10} +, \ldots \ldots \ldots \ldots, \mu_s y_{so} \ldots \ldots \ldots (9)$$

subject to $\quad v_1 x_{10} +, \ldots \ldots \ldots \ldots, v_m x_{mo} = 1$

$$\mu_1 y_{1j} +, \ldots \ldots \ldots, \mu_s y_{sj} \leq v_1 x_{1j} +, \ldots \ldots \ldots, v_m x_{mj} \ (j=1, 2....n)$$

$$v_1, v_2, v_3, \ldots \ldots v_m \geq 0$$

$$\mu_1, \mu_2, \ldots\ldots \mu_s, \geq 0$$

Suppose the optimal solution of the (LP_0) is (θ^*, u^*, v^*) *since* $v =, v^*$ *and* $u = \mu^*$ where $(u^*$ *and* $v^*)$ are values with constraints given in the (LP_0). The CCR efficiency for DMU_0

can be achieved if ($\theta^* = 1$ and there exists at least one optimal (with (u^*, v^*) with $v^* > 0$ *and* $u^* > 0$ otherwise the DMU_o inefficient. That is either $(\theta^* < 1)$ or $(\theta^* = 1)$ and at least one element of (u^*, v^*) is zero for every optimal solution. The DMUs that are fully efficient for a particular DMU_o are called the reference set or the peer group for the DMU_o. It is the existence of the collection of such efficient DMU forces the DMU_o to be inefficient.

However, the dual problem will allow the semi-positive data for (X, Y). This will also facilitate redefining the CCR-efficiency by taking into account the *input excesses* and *output shortfalls*. Since the CCR-model has two orientations, the *input oriented CCR* model tries to minimise the inputs while satisfying at least the given input levels. The *output oriented-CCR* model aims at maximising output without requiring more inputs of any one or of all observed ones.

In the matrix form the *Input Oriented CCR* model [Multiplier Form] is stated as

[Multiplier Form] (LP_o) $\max_{v,u} \quad u\, y_o$ ....(10)

Subject to

$$vx_o = 1$$

$$-vX + uY \leq 0$$

$$v \geq 0, u \geq 0$$

Here the v *and* u are input and output multipliers treated as variables. The Dual problem of the (LP_o) is

[Envelope Form] (DLP_o) $\min_{\theta,\lambda} \quad \theta$ ....(11)

Subject to

$$\theta x_o - X\lambda \leq 0$$

$$Y\lambda \geq y_o$$

$$\lambda \geq 0$$

The (DLP_o) has a solution (feasible, $\theta = 1, \lambda_o = 1, \lambda_j (j \neq 0)$. Therefore, the optimal θ^* cannot be greater than 1 and must be greater than zero. It means $0 < \theta \leq 1$. The DLP_o aims at to reduce the input vector radially to θx_0 so that the activity remains in the production possibility set keeping the output at least at the original level with this. The input excesses $s^- \in R^m$ and the output shortfall $s^- \in R^s$ can be defined as $s^- = \theta x_o - X\lambda$ *and* $s^+ = Y\lambda - y_o$ with s^- *and* $s^+ \geq 0$ for feasible solution. Further, to solve the DLF$_0$ by considering the *input excesses* and the *output shortfall*, there are two phase processes: the first phase aims at getting the optimal value of θ^* as specified in the DLF$_0$ and then in the second phase θ^* (Farrell Efficiency named after M. J Farrell, 1957) is incorporated in the maximisation problem as specified in the equation-12.

$$\max_{\lambda, s^-, s^+} \quad w = es^- + es^+ \ldots\ldots(12)$$

Subject to

$$s^- = \theta^* x_o - X\lambda$$
$$s^+ = Y\lambda - y_0$$

So this phase tries to maximise the sum of the *input excesses* and *output shortfall* while keeping the $\theta = \theta^*$. An optimal solution $(\theta^*, \lambda^*, s^{-*}, s^{+*})$ of the second phase is called the *Max-Slack Solution.* If s^{-*} *and* s^{+*} are zero then, they are *called zero slack.* Hence, if the optimal solution θ^*=1 and slacks are zero then the DMU$_0$ is called ***CCR-efficient otherwise inefficient.***

When θ^*=1 it is called ***Radial Efficiency or Technical Efficiency*** because $\theta^* < 1$ means all the inputs can be reduced simultaneously without changing the input mix. Any inefficiency related to input slack is called mix inefficiency. Hence, the radial efficiency (**Weak Efficiency**) and mix efficient together called ***Pareto Koopman efficiency or Strong efficiency.*** The above idea suggests that the efficiency of an inefficient unit can be improved by the radial contractions of input and elimination of input slack. Hence, the ***CCR-Projection*** (improvement)(equation- 13)

$$\hat{x}_o = \theta^* x_o - s^{-*} \leq x_o$$

$$\hat{y}_o = y_o + s^{+*} \geq y_o \ldots\ldots (13)$$

2.4.2. BCC Model of DEA Method

Since the beginning of the DEA model (CCR-Model) many extensions have been made and BCC (Banker, Charnes and Cooper) is one which is the most representative. The BCC model has its production frontier spanned by the convex Hull of the existing DMUs. The frontier have piece-wise linear and concave characteristics that leads to Variable Returns to Scale (VRS): that is increasing Returns to scale (IRS) in the beginning; decreasing returns to scale (DRS) in the second segment and Constant Returns to Scale (CRS) in the transition. *The input oriented BCC* model evaluates the efficiency of the DMU_o by solving the envelopment form shown in equation-14.

$$\min_{\theta_{B,\lambda}} \quad \theta_B \ldots\ldots\ldots\ldots\ldots\ldots\ldots\ldots (14)$$

Subject to

$$\begin{aligned} \theta_B x_o - X\lambda &\geq 0 \\ Y\lambda &\geq y_0 \\ e\lambda &= 1 \\ \lambda &\geq 0 \end{aligned}$$

$$e\lambda = \sum_{j=1}^{n} \lambda_j = 1 \text{ where } \theta_B \text{ is a scalar}$$

The primal problem (BCC_o) is solved using two phase procedure similar to the CCR two phase process. In the first phase we minimise and in the second phase, we maximise the sum of the slacks. The optimal solution $(\theta^*_{B,} \lambda^*, s^{-*}, s^{+*})$ is ***BCC efficient*** if $\theta^*_{B,} = 1$ and all the slacks are Zero, otherwise the DMU under evaluation is inefficient. Both input and output orientation is considered simultaneously by the additive model in the form of single scalar called SBM (Slack based measure) which has been introduced by Tone (1997, 2001).

2.5. Output Oriented Model

In the input oriented model, we have been dealing mainly with models to minimise inputs while producing at least the given output level. This model is known as the input oriented model. Under the output oriented model we want to maximise outputs while using no more than the observed amount of any input. As per Cooper et. al., (2005, p. 58), the Dual Linear Programming of Output Orientation (DLPO) can be specified as following

$$DLPO_o = \max_{\eta,\mu} \eta$$

$$\text{Subject to } x_o - X\mu \geq 0$$

$$\eta y_o - Y\mu \leq 0 \quad \ldots\ldots (15)$$

$$\mu \geq 0$$

An optimal solution of $DLPO_o$ can be derived directly from an optimal solution of the input oriented CCR model specified in equation 9 and 10. If we define $\lambda = {}^{\mu}/_{\eta}, \theta = {}^{1}/_{\eta}$ then $DLPO_o$ becomes

$$DLP_o \min_{\theta,\lambda} \theta$$

$$\text{Subject to} \quad \theta x_o - X\lambda \geq 0 \quad \ldots\ldots (16)$$

$$y_o - Y\lambda \leq 0$$

$$\lambda \geq 0$$

This is the input Oriented CCR model. Hence, the solution of the output oriented model relates to that of input oriented model via $\eta^* = {}^{1}/_{\theta^*}, \mu^* = {}^{\lambda^*}/_{\theta^*}$ This shows that the output oriented efficiency score is the inverse of the input oriented efficiency score in the CCR model as it assumes constant returns to scale. The slack of the output oriented model (t^-, t^+) is

$$X\mu + t^- = x_o$$

$$Y\mu - t^+ = \eta y_0$$

Hence, $t^{-*} = {}^{s^{-*}}/_{\theta^*}$, $t^{+*} = {}^{s^{+*}}/_{\theta^*}$. Hence if $\theta^* \leq 1$ then $\eta^* \geq 1$.

The higher the value $\eta^*$of the less efficient is the DMU. The value expresses the output enlargement rate. The DEA analysis presented in chapter 4 specially focuses on the equation 15.

2.6. Super Efficiency DEA Model

The model is proposed by Anderson and Peterson (1993). The efficiency scores from these models are obtained by eliminating the data on the DMU_o to be evaluated from the solution set. The CCR model of Super efficiency (SE) is specified as

$$\theta^* = \min_{\theta,\lambda s^- s^+} \theta - \varepsilon e s^+ \qquad (17)$$

Subject to

$$\theta x_o = \sum_{j=1,\neq 0}^{n} \lambda_j x_j + s^-$$

$$y_o \sum_{j=1,\neq 0}^{n} \lambda_j y_j - s^+$$

$\lambda, s^+, s^-$are constrained to be non-negative. $\varepsilon > 0$ is the usual non-Archmedian element and e is the row vector with unity in all elements. This model is used in order to get the rankings of the CCR efficient DMUs who are assigned the score of ones. However, the model suffers from infeasibility problem. Therefore, the alternative models such as the SBM (Slack Based Measure) model (Cooper *et. al.*, p. 308) with output oriented constant returns to scale assumption is used in the analysis. The model is specified as follows:

$$\delta_o^* = \min_{\psi,\ \lambda} \frac{1}{1-1/s\sum_{r=1}^{s}\psi r} \qquad (18)$$

$$\sum_{j=1,\neq o}^{n} x_{ij}\lambda_j \leq x_o (i = 1, \ldots \ldots, m)$$

$$\sum_{j=1,\neq o}^{n} y_{rj}\lambda_j + y_{ro}\psi_r \geq y_{ro} (r = 1, \ldots \ldots, s)$$

$$\psi_r \geq 0 \text{ for all } r \text{ and } \lambda_j \geq 0 \text{ for all } j$$

Chapter - 3

Sikkim University in the Context of Education System in India

3.1. University Education in India

In India 'university' means university established or incorporated by or under a Central Act, Provincial Act or State Act and includes any such institutions as may, in consultation with the university concerned, be recognised by the University Grants Commission (UGC) in accordance with the regulation made in this regard under the UGC Act, 1956. At present the main categories of university/ university level institutions are: central Universities, State Universities, Deemed to be Universities and University level institutions. The central universities are established by Central Act.

Higher education is the shared responsibilities both at the centre and the states. The coordination and determination of standards of universities and colleges is entrusted to the UGC and other statutory regulatory bodies. As per the reports of Ministry of Human Resource Development (MHRD), Government of India (GOI), the number of universities has increased 34 times from 20 in 1950 to 677 in 2014. Out of these 45 central universities, 40 are under the perview of the MHRD, 318 state universities, 185 state private universities, 129 Deemed to be universities and 51 institutions of national importance (16 IITs, 30 NITs and 5 IISERs).

National Assessment and Accreditation Council (NAAC), an autonomous body has been established by the UGC in 1994 in presence of the recommendations made by The National Policy of Education, 1986 and the Programme of Action (POA), 1992 which lay special emphasis on evaluating the quality of higher education in India. Its prime mandate is to access and accredit institutions of higher learning and universities.

The India Higher education system has undergone rapid expansion. In less than 20 years the country has created additional capacity for a mammoth 40 million students. While the scale of this expansion is remarkable in itself, what sets it apart from earlier decades of equally aggressive expansion in a deliberate strategy and on organised design?

In recent years the country has undertaken massive structural and systematic changes that have started to yield encouraging outcome. About 15 years ago, India consciously moved to a differentiated academic system with a three tired structure comprising highly selective elite research universities at the top, comprehensive universities and specialised institutions in the middle and an array of highly accessible and high quality colleges at the bottom.

Indian Higher education system has undergone massive expansion to become the largest in the world enrolling over 70 million students. Such expansion would have been unimaginable without the extensive use of Information and Communication Technology (ICT).Online platforms and ICT tools have helped take higher education to millions of deserving students in far-flung areas who would otherwise have no access to university education. Online education has become the first part of call for many students who were earlier left out of the higher education system or had to settle for lower quality alternatives. Technology has not only been instrumental in addressing the demand-supply gap for quality education, but has fundamentally changed the nature of several educational process. In short, technology has been nothing short of disruptive for Indian higher education, solving for three India's pressing problems–access, equity and quality- at once.

3.2. Initiatives by UGC On Higher Education

The Higher Education Institutions (HEI) is the bigger contributor to India's academic research output. In this context, the ranking of the university provides an indicator of quality, efficiency and competitiveness. The First Global University Rankings became available in 2003 when Sanghai Jiao Jong university published the results in the form of academic ranking of world universities (ARWU), where three Indian institutions appeared in the world's rankings in 2003 (IISC, Bangalore), in 251-300 bracket and IIT Delhi and Kharagpur in the 451-500 bracket. The rankings are based on research in the indicators. In 2013, sixteen out of 20 research organisations of Indian ranking by output (SIR Global Indian, 2013) belonged to this sector.

A conference of Vice Chancellors of Central and State universities, held on March 25-26, 2011, reviewed the achievements during the Eleventh Five Year Plan and the agenda for the Twelfth Plan was published by the UGC as university and Society: Issues and Challenges edited by Prof. Ved Prakash, the Chairman of UGC.

It was reiterated that higher education played a vital role in the development process in the context of 'Knowledge' based economy. The close connectedness of the world's economy becomes crucial for India to have an equal and qualitative access to higher education at affordable rate. The main issues of discussions were centered on:

- Access, equality, engagement and outcomes;
- Content and quality;
- Research and innovations;
- The way research programme such as M.Phil and PhDs were organised and carried out;
- Time and energy devoted by the faculties in implementing independent research projects;
- Outcome and quality of research undertaken by faculties and researchers;

- Integrating research and teaching;
- Faculty development and inter university resource sharing;
- Internationalisation in higher education;
- Alternative mode of delivery of higher education;
- Models of financing higher education;
- Proposed chair in the name of Nobel Laureates;
- Inter-University centre for teacher education;
- Immigration of knowledge and skill;
- Implementation of Community College scheme;
- Good Governance;
- Augmenting human resources for enhanced efficiency;
- Working Group for Higher education in the Twelve Five Year Plan;
- *Rastriya Uchattara Siksha Abhiyan*, and
- Entrusting UGC with New responsibilities.

While much has been done towards ensuring quality, instituting accountability, enabling private participation, promoting internationalisation and so on, there are five salient trends that deserve particular mention when talking of governance reform since 2013. First, over the years, the government has gradually withdrawn from direct management of public institutions revolving governance to boards comprising academics, alumni and external members self-regulation and self-critique has become the norm. The government's role as a provider of funding has also seen some shapes. Secondly, there is moving from monitoring inputs to regulating outcomes. The move towards regulating outcomes has been accompanied by the introduction of more sophisticated quality assurance system based on establishment of a National accreditation agency for higher education and several other agencies with a specialised focus. Further, there is serious effort made towards enabling environment for private and foreign participation.

However, the higher education system in India faces the challenges such as India's Gross Enrolment Ratio (GER) of 16 per cent was much below the world average of 27 per cent as well as that of other emerging countries such as China (26 per cent) and Brazil (36 per cent) in 2010. There is faculty shortage (40 per cent and 35 per cent respectively) in state and central universities. 60 per cent of the universities and 90 per cent of the colleges were average or below average in 2010 on the basis of NAAC accreditation. There is wide disparity in the GER of higher education across states and the gross attendance ratio in urban and rural area.

3.3. Sikkim University

Central University of Sikkim (hereafter CUS) was constituted under the Sikkim University Act 2006 (10 of 2007) and came into existence on July 2, 2007. As per the Fifth Annual Report (2011-12) the university has the following objectives:

1. To disseminate and advance knowledge by providing instructional and research facilities in such branches of learning as it may deem fit;
2. To take appropriate measures for promoting innovations in teaching- learning process, inter-disciplinary studies and research;
3. To educate and train manpower for the development of the state of Sikkim;
4. To pay special attention to the improvement of the socio-economic conditions and welfare of the people of the state; their intellectual, academic and cultural development.

CUS fulfils a long cherished aspiration of not just the people of Sikkim to have a national level higher institution of learning. Its mission is to contribute substantially to the nation building process by

1. Mobilising the rich intellectual heritage of this region;

2. Galvanising the academic fervour and creative instincts of youth; and
3. Developing agencies and institutions that will facilitate cross boarder interactions.

CUS is trying to bring the best practices of academic programme teaching methods and curriculum design both from and within and outside India. The first executive council of CUS was constituted vide Government of India, MHRD Notification No. F.36-4/2007 Desk (U) dated 21st February, 2008. The 2nd Executive Council was constituted Vide MHRD, GOI Notification No. 36-9/2011 Desk (U) dated on 04 January 2012.

The First Academic Council of CUS was constituted vide Notification No. F. 36-4/2008 Desk (U) dated 16th July 2008. It is the principal academic body of the university which coordinates and exercises general supervision over the academic policies of the university.

Table 3.1: Faculty Strengths under Different Schools

Name of the School	*No. of Depts*	*No. of Asstt. Prof*	*No. of Asst. Prof*	*No. of Prof*
Social Sciences	7	17	4	-
Life Sciences	9	23	4	1
Language	4	7	1	1
Human Sciences	3	6	2	-
Professional Studies	6	10	1	-

Note: These figures include only the permanent faculties. All the guest faculties are not included. As per the 8th Annual report (2014-15), the University has six schools consisting of all together 29 departments.

Out of 29 departments, 13 departments have only PG programme (Anthropology, Chinese, Computer Application, Education, English, Geology, Hindi, Law, MBA, Mathematics, Tourism and Zoology); only one department has PG and MPhil programme (Chemistry); two departments Commerce and Psychology have PG and PhD programme. Rest 13 departments (Economics, Botany, Geography, History, International Relation, Mass Communication, Microbiology, Nepali, Peace and Conflict Studies and Management and Sociology,

Horticulture, Physics and Political Science). In addition to this, 12 colleges (six government and six private colleges) are affiliated to Sikkim University. As per the Annual Report (2014-15) a total of 822 students were enrolled into different courses and the total faculty strength was 120. The current year expenditure (2014-15) under the heading of general fund is Rs. '280,856,407. The break-ups of the total is furnished in the Table: 3.2 given below.

Table-3.2 Break-ups of the Total Expenditure under the General Fund

Components	Rs.
Staff payments and benefits	162963960
Academic Expenses	43445822
Administrative and General Expenses	67517298
Transportation Expenses	4729463
Repair and maintenance	2185823
Finance Cost	14041
Total	**280,856,407**

Source: Sikkim University.

The Eighth Annual Report shows that the total number of students admitted in the year 2014-15 is 822. In order to compute the expenditure incurred by the university on each department (not directly available in the Annual Accounts Report of Sikkim University), the per capita student expenditure was calculated by dividing the total expenditure by the total no. of students admitted in that year. Then the expenditure on each department was estimated by multiplying the per capita student expenditure with the no. of students enrolled. As far as the area in square feet utilised by each department is concerned, the official reports have been accessed from the University. However, for some department the data were missing and the approximations have been made on the basis of the rooms utilised by the department under consideration.

Table 3.3: Details of the Department-wise Performance of the Students in Examination

Deptt.	*Total passed*	*1st div*	*2nd Div*	*3rd Div*	*Avg Marks*	*Avg score of Male student*	*Avg score of Female student*	*No. of male (no of female)*
Law	14	7	7	-	60.2	59	60	2(12)
Antro	8	8	-	-	67	65	70	4(4)
Chin	1	1	-	-	-	77	77	1
Eco	19	4	10	5	57	53	59	6(13)
Edu	23	22	1	-	70.4	70.4	70.5	5(18)
Eng	23	7	14	2	57	56	57	4(19)
Geog	25	10	15	-	59	56.7	60.1	11(14)
Hind	11	9	2	-	65	63.8	66	4(7)
Hist	26	21	5	-	65.2	64.5	65.6	9(17)
IR	12	5	5	2	57	55.8	59.5	8(4)
Masc	6	6	-	-	68.2	67.4	68.5	2(4)
Nep	35	25	10	-	62	59.3	62.3	8(27)
Pcm	10	4	6	-	60	61	60.1	6(4)
Psc	23	3	18	2	55	55.1	54.7	9(14)
Soc	26	13	12	1	60	59.1	60.3	5(21)
Tour	21	12	7	2	60.3	52.5	63	6(15)
Mang	22	22	-	-	71	70.3	70.2	7(15)
Comm	24	18	5	1	63	60.3	64.2	11(13)
Bot	15	14	1	-	72	71.3	73	6(9)
Chem	14	10	4	-	66	64	68	9(6)
Geol	10	10	-	-	73	69.5	78.7	7(3)
Math	1	8	2	1	67.1	63.8	73.1	9(2)
Micb	16	11	4	1	64	67	61.2	7(9)
Phy	15	9	5	1	62	61	64.5	11(4)
Psy	7	6	1	-	71	-	71	(7)
Zool	11	10	1	-	70	64.8	75.5	6(5)
Hort	15	15	-	-	74	72.2	75.2	6(9)

Note: The names of the department are given in the short form. There is no distinction between small and capital letters for the departments. They are used synonymously.

In relation to the division scored, there are Nine departments in which all the students have got 1st divisions (60 per cent and above) are Law, Antro, Chin, Edu, Masc, Bot, Zool and Hort. In ten departments the scores have been distributed from 1st divisions to 3rd Divisions. Rest of the Departments of the all 27 departments have the range between 1st and 2nd divisions. This is to be mentioned here that department of Computer Application is not included as it does not have the master programme (Table 3.3)

The gender-wise distribution of the students across the departments shows that only seven departments have number of boys more than the corresponding girls' figure (Zool, Phy, Math, Geol, Chem, Pcm and IR). Rest 20 departments have more girls than the boys. On an average, the performance of the girls in terms of average marks is more than the average scores of the boys. In case of Science subjects such as Math, Phy, Zool, Chem Geol more number of boys are admitted compared to girls. However, the performances of girls compared to boys in those subjects are comparatively more. Psychology is the only subjects which does not have boys enrolment. On the basis of the average marks scored by the departments (in per cent), all the departments can be grouped into two category (less than equal to 60 per cent and above 60 per cent)

Table 3.4: Groupings of the Departments on the Basis of the Average Marks of Department

Average marks	*Name of Departments*
Less Than equal to 60 per cent	Law, Eco, Eng, Geog, IR, Pcm, Psc, Soc (8)
Above 60 per cent	Antro, Chin, Edu, Hind, Hist, Masc, Nep and Tour, Mang,Comm, Bot,Chem, Geol, Math, Micb, Psy, Phy, Zool and Hort (19)

This Table 3.4 shows that the performance of the students in the Arts stream in comparison to Arts stream is low. However, the language courses help the students to score better and consequently there are more 1st divisions. The reasons may be

- Lack of sound background and concrete foundation at the UG level courses hinders the students to cope with the PG courses quickly as the PG courses are relatively more advanced.
- Most often as the students share in the classroom that the actual teaching course in the class is actually not many times covered in the syllabus. The teacher most often covers the basic things without covering the actual syllabus. Therefore the delivery of

knowledge from the syllabus to the students seems to be immaterial.

- Lack of teaching infrastructure at UG level.
- Negligence of the students in attending the classes. Strict attendance must be adhered to enforce study habit among the students.
- Crash Courses in subjects who requires some technical skill or mathematical knowledge.
- Availability of textbooks in multiple copies for each subject. Many times students do not get a book as there is only one copy or few copies are available in the library.
- Strict adherence to the quality teaching should be made. A rational mechanism for monitoring quality teaching should be placed in the system.
- Weekly anonymous students feedback directly to the Honourable VC office regarding the coverage of course, quality of teaching, method of teaching and teachers' punctuality.
- The classrooms should be strictly under the monitoring of live cameras which should be directly connected to the Honourable VC's Office. This will definitely improve the quality of teaching and punctuality. Further, the feedback of the student can be verified from that video.
- Location of the departments and accessibility to central library should be given prior importance.
- More financial autonomy should be given to the purchase of textbooks and Journals for the library.
- The UG teachers at various colleges under the Sikkim University should be provided basic appraisal of the courses taught at the university so that there will be uniformity and symmetry in teaching.

Chapter - 4

Analysis and Interpretation of the Results

On the basis of the objectives of the study the methods have been outlined (Chapter 1) secondary data have been collected to compute the results. As specifically mentioned in the methodology chapter, basically there are three methods such as CCR, BCC and the Super Efficiency (SE) models have been used to compute the department specific efficiency levels on the basic of the inputs and outputs that have been defined in methodology chapter. Further, on the basis of the output oriented methods, both *Farrell Efficiency* and *Pareto-Koopman Efficiency* (Weak and Strong Efficiency) have been computed with the projections of the in-efficient departments on the basis of input and output slacks. The formation of virtual department which is regarded as the efficient department for the inefficient one is analysed the importance of the input and output weights determined in the process of the analysis will be interpreted with reference to the context of efficiency. Lastly, the ranking of the fully efficient department (not made under the CCR and BCC method) are computed in order to estimate the rankings of the fully efficient DMUs.

4.1. Results of CCR Output Oriented Model

On the basis of the Eighth Annual Reports (2014-15) of Sikkim University, there are 29 departments functioning in the university. However, in order to make the homogeneity in the departments (Now onwards the department will be treated as DMU as frequently used in the DEA literature), 27 departments have been considered excluding Computer Application and Music as these two departments do not run PG courses. Hence, the analysis is based on all the 27 departments which have PG and higher courses like MPhil and PhD courses.

As per equation-4 the CCR efficiency of each DMU has been computed using three outputs and five inputs. The outputs of the university are the total scores (consisting of the publication of national and international research articles, major or minor projects, conferences attended, no. of lectures delivered, no. of M.Phil and PhD students registered, conferences organised and teachers training attained), average marks of all the students who have passed, no. of 1st divisions and the inputs are the area utilised by the DMU, no. of permanent faculties, total expenditure incurred on each DMU, No. of female students and no. of male students enrolled under the DMU.

Table 4.1: Descriptive Statistics of the Input -Outputs of the CCR model

Items	*AREA*	*NPF*	*TEX*	*NFS*	*NMS*	*TRS*	*AM*	*NFD*
MAX	11490	6	2 crores	27	11	535	74	25
MIN	2500	2	20 lakhs	1	0	1	55	1
MEAN	4986	4	92 lakhs	10.3	6.25	191.6	64.5	10.7
SD	**1963**	**1.41**	**46 lakhs**	**6.45**	**2.9**	**137.9**	**5.39**	**6.16**

Note: NPF-No. of permanent faculties; TEX total expenditure; NFS no. of female students; NMS- No. of male students; TRS- Teachers' research score; AM average marks of the students of the department, NFD- No. of first divisions.

The information from the Table 4.1 shows that there is a huge variation in the minimum and maximum numbers in case of all the inputs and outputs. The correlation Table 6 provides information on the partial correlation between inputs and outputs.

Table 4.2: Partial Correlation Matrix of Inputs and Outputs under CCR Model

Inputs\ Outputs	*Area*	*NPF*	*TEX*	*NFS*	*NMS*	*TRS*	*AM*	*FD*
Area	1	0.58057	0.121040	-0.07679	0.41924	0.18857	0.17993	0.14469
NPF	0.58057	1	0.495908	0.34065	0.53267	0.54290	-0.17873	0.29750
TEX	0.12104	0.49590	1	0.65739	0.36902	0.41678	-0.50612	0.26642
NFS	-0.07679	0.34065	0.657396	1	0.17333	0.16525	-0.33146	0.63228
NMS	0.41924	0.53267	0.369025	0.17333	1	0.27195	-0.25832	0.33736
TRS	0.18857	0.54290	0.41678	0.16525	0.27195	1	-0.38584	0.00572
AM	0.17993	-0.17873	-0.50612	-0.33146	-0.25832	-0.38584	1	0.335076
NFD	0.144691	0.297509	0.266423	0.632285	0.337367	0.005725	0.335076	1

As per this Table 4.2, the correlation matrix brings out the relationship between any two variables keeping others constant. There is a positive correlation between Area and number of permanent faculties. Total expenditure is also positively correlated to the number of permanent faculties. TRS is positively correlated to the number of permanent faculties. However, the AM and total expenditure shows a negative correlation. This indicates increasing in expenditure does not lead to increase in performance of the students. It may be due to the fact that the allocation of time of faculties between teaching and research is more favourable towards research activities.

However, increasing number of first divisions is correlated to total expenditure. The economic reasoning may be that the increase in the number of 1st divisions are comparatively less in numbers in a class, hence the average marks becomes less.

There has to be clear cut distinction between research and teaching activities. If both research and teaching are to increase, the focus should be given more on the recruitment of the permanent faculties so that faculties can concentrate on teaching as well as research. It is noteworthy that in JNU the total number of faculties as per 2011 was 473 which is around four times that of CUS. The teacher student ratio is 1:15.5.(accessed from www.jnu.ac.in statistical fact sheet of JNU). There is an indication that the 1st divisions and the no of girls' students are correlated to a greater extent. Table 4.2a presents the vital information of all the CCR and BCC models in all the three cases. The number of fully efficient DMUs declined as the number of merging of DMUs increased. Secondly, the mean efficiency drastically declined in third case. PCM and Edu remained peers in all the three cases and PCM is considered to be the largest number of times preferred DMU by the inefficient DMUs. The additional information on descriptive statistics of Case 2 and Case 3 are presented in the appendix (at the end).

Table 4.2a: Vital Statistics of the CCR and BCC models in all the Three Cases

	Case 1		*Case-2*		*Case-3*	
	CCR	*BCC*	*CCR*	*BCC*	*CCR*	*BCC*
No. of DMU	27	27	25	25	22	22
Output	3	3	3	3	2	2
Inputs	5	5	5	5	5	5
Mean eff.	0.909	0.961	0.911	0.949	0.818	0.896
S.D	0.146	0.063	0.139	0.09	0.17	0.133
No. of fully eff. DMU	17	18	15	17	7	10
No. of inefficient DMU	10	9	10	8	15	12
Freq. of peers	PCM-8, Edu-5, Geol-4	Psy-5, Edu-5, Geol-5 Hort-5	PCM-7, Hind-6, Edu-5	PCM-5, Geog-4, Edu-4	PCM-10, Psy-10, Hind-9, Edu-4	Hind-11, Pcm-7, Psy-6, Mang-3

As per the CCR –output oriented results, the DMUs on the frontier (CCR-efficient DMUs) are 17 in number and they are: Tour, Masc, Hist, Mang, Law, PCM, Edu, Psy, Antro, Hort, Micb, Zool, Nepa, Geol, Math, Hind and Chin. All these DMUs have CCR- score of 1 as per the observed inputs and outputs used in the analysis.

Out of total 27 DMUs, 17 DMUs are fully CCR efficient and 10 DMUs are below the frontier meaning that they have the chance/opportunities to improve the output without changing the input mix. The mean efficiency score is 0.9098 that is there is possibility that on an average 10 per cent of the current output can be increased with the existing input when compared to the efficient DMUs. Under the CCR-output oriented model the maximum score is 1 and the DMU is said to be fully efficient and the minimum score is 0.517 which is the score of PSC.

The relatively less efficient DMUs are 10 in number and they are: (CCR score less than 1 and greater than zero) are classified into four categories as presented in Table 4.3.

Table 4.3: Classification of the Inefficient-DMUs on the Basis of the CCR-Score

Efficiency scores class	*DMUs(score)*	*No*
90%	Bot (.933), Phy(0.931), Eco (.90)	3
80% to less than 90%	Comm	1
70% and less than 80%	Soc (0.786), Che (0.769), IR (0.79)	3
50% and less than 69%	**Eng (0.618) Geog (0.55) and Psc (0.517)**	**3**

The analysis of the DMUs whose score lies between 90 per cent and less than 1, then Bot can improve its output by 7 per cent. The projection of the input output results shows that in order to bring on to the frontier by improving the NFD by 7.15 per cent that is from 14 to 15, AM by 10.33 per cent from 72 per cent to 79 per cent and TRS by 7.14 per cent that is from 125 to 133. Since, the inputs changes are not within the total control of the DMU, the focus is on the output expansion and hence, the output oriented model is used for the analysis.

Since Bot is inefficient as far as the CCR technology is concerned, it follows some of or all of the fully efficient DMUs to be its peer whose structure of input-output relation can be adopted to become more efficient. The Table 4.4 shows the weights (lambda) of the peers for the inefficient DMUs.

Table 4.4: The Weights of the Peers for Each In-efficient DMUs

DMUs	*Reference/peers Group with Weight(ë)*
Bot	0.291(Geol)+0.572(Antr)+0.434(Mang)+0.344(Masc)
Eco	0.866(PCM)+0.393(Psy)+0.133(Tour)
Phy	0.504(PCM)+0.145(Geol)+0.772(Math)

From the Table 4.4, it can be conferred that Bot can be fully CCR efficient if it can form a virtual DMU with a combination of 29 per cent of Geol, 57.2 per cent of Antro, 43 per cent of Mang and 34 per cent of Masc's output. Similarly, Phy can be projected onto the efficient production frontier if it combines PCM, Geol and Math in 50.4 per cent, 14.5 per cent and 77.2 per cent respectively. Eco considers PCM Psy and Tour as the peers with the weights 86.6 per cent, 39.3 per cent and 13.3 per cent respectively.

The reference group of the DMU within the range of CCR scores (80 per cent and less than 90 per cent) are represented in the Table 4.5.

Table 4.5: The Weights of the Peers for Each In-efficient DMUs (50 per cent to less than 90 per cent)

DMUs	*Peer Groups (with ë)*	*CCR*	*Score Projection output*
Comm	1.03 (Geol)+0.55 (Edu)	0.802	72.59, 81.10, 24.6
SOC	.220(Law) +.133(PCM) +.24(Hind) +.558(EDU)	0.786	27.18, 27.18, 27.18
Chem	.029(PCM)+.288(Zool)+.102(Math) +.726(Hind)+.105(Edu)	.769	30.02, 30.02, 30.02
IR	.737(PCM)+.154(Geol)+.272(Math) +.0406(Chin)	.744	34.28, 34.28, 34.28
Eng	.392(PCM)+.677(Psy)+.199(Edu) +.107(Tour)	.618	61.74, 61.74, 61.74
Geog	1.03(PCM)+.352(Zool)+.145(Antro) +.417(Edu)	.555	80.16, 113.52, 80.16
PSC	.71(PCM)+.412(Hind)+.0826(Psy) +.51(Tour)	517	93.3, 93.3, 3.40

The last column of the Table 4.5 shows the output projections under CCR output oriented model for the three outputs such as TRS, AM and NFD. PSC has been ranked as the lowest efficient DMU among all the 27 DMUs analysed under CCR model. The output projection shows the extent of expansion of the outputs without changing the input ratio to attain full efficiency. (Three per cent of the existing outputs can be expanded without increasing the inputs. IT adopts PCM, Hind, Psy and Tour as the Peers for attaching the weights of increasing the output. Among these DMUs the minimum expansion of output is 27 per cent (for Soc) and Maximum expansion is 93 per cent (for PSC).

In case of the second output (AM) the minimum expansion is 27.18 per cent for SOC and maximum of 113.52 per cent for Geog. For 3rd output (NFD) the minimum expansion is 24.6 per cent (for Comm) and maximum expansion is 340 per cent for PSC. The scores are CCR score (input Oriented). The output Oriented CCR score is inverse of CCR input oriented score.

4.2. Output Weights of the Inefficient DMUs Under CCR Model

The following Table 4.6 shows the output weights. The output weights are actually reflects the reduction in the cost per unit increase in the output. This will guide for the actual policy formulation on different output that are to be produced by the DMUs.

Table-4.6: Output Weights and Weighted Data of the Inefficient DMUs under CCR Model

DMUs	u_1	u_2	u_3	u_1y_1	u_2y_2	u_3y_3
Eco	.000401	.0147	0	.16019	.8398	0
IR	.00181	.00183	.083	.518	.0649	.416
Psc	.000230	.0173	0	.0481	.9518	0
Soc	.00142	.00855	.02142	.02080	.513	.278
Bot	0	0	.0714	0	0	1
Chem	.00113	.00342	.0661	.1137	.2257	.660
Phy	.00148	0	.0708	.363	0	.63
Eng	.000541	.0150	.00170	.0969	.853	.0497
Geog	.000874	0	.0685	.3146	0	.685
Comm	0	0	.0556	.0506	.852	.0966

The benefit (or reduction in the cost) of increasing output by one unit is indicated by the output weights. The more is the weight; the better is the demand for that output. This also reflects the scarcity or shortage of the output. For Eco, the contribution of AM is 83 per cent where as the contribution of TRS is only 16 per cent. Further, it gives zero weight to the NFD. Hence, increasing the performance has to be given more weight in order to improve its efficiency score.

4.3.1. Economics

4.3.1.1. CCR and BCC model, 1st Case

After examining the overall picture under the CCR model, it is time now to go for department specific analysis under CCR and BCC models and applying different situations. This to be mentioned that there are three alternative situations (Cases) have been considered while applying the DEA model. These are (1), 27 departments have been evaluated with 5 inputs and 3 outputs as specified earlier; (2), Two most smallest departments (Math and Tour) has been merged with Phy and Geog to see the impact of the merging on other efficient and inefficient DMUs, and (3), the 25 DMUs with two outputs (TRS and AM) and four inputs (male and female students have been merged into Total students). In addition to this for each of the three cases two different types of technology adopted (CCR and BCC). The CCR model assumes the constant Returns to scale and the BCC model allows Variable returns to scale i.e., all the three (CRS, IRS, DRS). The benefit of using both CCR and BCC model (as mentioned in the Methodology chapter) is to calculate the scale of operation and to find the *Most Productive Scale and Size* DMU (MPSS).

As far as the CCR model is concerned, in the case 1, out of 27 DMUs 17 DMUs became fully efficient (CCR Score=1) and 10 DMUs became inefficient. Eco has been ranked 19th out of 27 with a score of (1.102=1/0.907) and ranked 3 among the inefficient DMUs followed by Bot and Phy. Looking at the weights of the output, it can be said that the DMU under consideration gives 16 per cent weight to the first output and 84 per cent to the second output. As far as the output projection is concerned it has the capacity to increase the output, on an average by 10.23 per cent and the projected output is 440 from 399 increasing by 10.24 per cent (TRS), AM to increase by 10.24 per cent (from 57 to 63) and the third output by 32.56 per cent (from 4 to 5.3). This suggests that as the weight for NFD is zero, the DMU does not have any cost or benefit in expanding the output. Hence more percentage has been assigned to that output.

The reference set of the DMU indicates the weight that has to be given while forming a virtual DMU which will be fully efficient. It considers PCM, Psy and Tour as the peer group and produce on the frontier as the peers with a weight of 86 per cent, 4 per cent and 13 per cent respectively. This virtual DMU will be capable of expanding the present output by 10.23 per cent more.

However, the CCR model is used under the assumption of CRS. To examine the efficiency under VRS technology, the BCC model is used with same input output combinations. The mean efficiency score (BCC score is 0.925 with a SD (Standard Deviation) of 0.1326. This is more than the CCR mean score (=0.909). This implies that the DMU works well under the local environment and its efficiency gets improved when compared only to those DMUs who work in the similar situation instead of comparing all the DMUs. Compared to CCR model, the minimum BCC score has also increased from 0.517 to 0.555 and number of fully efficient DMUs increased to 18. Under the BCC model Eco operated more efficiently but the rank did not change from the CCR rank. Fortunately, it became second in the ranking among the inefficient DMUs. The Scale efficiency score is 0.950 (0.907/.954). The projection of scale efficiency is CRs. That is the DMU can expand its output and will experience CRS. The expansion of inputs can proportionately increase the output. Hence, focus should be given expansion of all inputs in existing proportion. Under, the BCC model, the peers group does not change but the weights has been changed to 78.4 per cent of PCM, 4.54 per cent of Psy and 17 per cent of Tour.

4.3.1.2. CCR and BCC Model under the Second case

Two DMUs Math and Tour have been merged with Phy and Geog respectively on the basis that there are no permanent faculties in Math and sine these two DMUs are smallest as far as the operation is concerned, they have been merged to the related DMUs so that the consequences of merging on the Phy and Geog as well as on other DMUs can be explained.

The Table 4.7 produces important results for Eco under the three different cases using both CCR and BCC model (output oriented) under the three different situations: in the first case five inputs and three outputs are used to evaluate the CCR and BCC efficiency and ranking of each DMU (27 DMUs). In the second case, Tour and Math are merged with Geog and Phy respectively to see if there is any impact of the merging of the DMUs as far as the smallest output are concerned. In the third case five DMUs such as Law with Psc, Geol with Chem, Math with Phy, Chin with Eng and Tour with Geog are merged. The merging decision is considered, because these DMUs have very low inputs in comparison to the other DMUs. Since DEA analysis considers a DMU to be more efficient which uses less inputs and produces more output, the care has been taken to see that the all the DMUs whose input used are very less not because of the production relation but because of the constraints due to policy decision of the University. These DMUs have very little amount of permanent faculties and they hire visiting faculties to run the courses. Since those temporary faculties only takes the teaching activity without any contribution to the research and other academic activities their number have not been considered. Therefore, merging of these small DMUs are thought to be merged with related DMUs to see if there is any change in the rankings, scores, and the reference group as well as the projection of output.

The Table 4.7 shows that under the 1st case the efficiency score has been has reduced from 1.102 (output oriented) to 1.086 when the CCR and BCC model is used. The rank also reduced from 20 to 21. In the CCR model the DMU under evaluation (Eco) gives a projection of 10.24 per cent, 10.24 per cent and 32.56 per cent for the three outputs

Table 4.7: The Details of the Results of Eco under Three Different Cases

Items	*1st case*		*2nd case*		*3rd case*	
	CCR	*BCC*	*CCR*	*BCC*	*CCR*	*BCC*
Rank (score)	20(1.102)	21(1.086)	18(1.09)	19 (1.08)	9(1.09)	13(1.08)
Reference Group	Pcm-86.67, psy-3.9, tour-13.3	Pcm-81.57, psy-5.2, edu-13.1	Pcm-83.28, hind-18.93	Pcm-82.92, geog-0.23, psy-16.83	Pcm-83.30, psy-17.19	Pcm-83.2, hind-0.44, psy-16.35
Inputs/ Outputs/No	5, 3, 27	5, 3, 27	5, 3, 25	5, 3, 25	5, 2, 22	5, 2, 22
Projection (slack)	10.24, 10.24, 32.56 (.892)	8.68, 8.68, 61.84, (2.126)	9.27, 9.27, 25.90, (.665)	8.76, 8.76, 9.48	9.11, 9.11	8.98, 8.98
Weight	16.01, 83.98, 0	14.68, 85.31, 0	10.9, 89.09, 0	13.83, 86.16, 0	10.17, 89.82	11.55, 88.44
RTS		CRS		DRS		CRS

respectively and in addition to this radial expansion there is shortage of the 3rd output slack which is figured out to be around 1 unit. Hence, the DMU can be projected on to the frontier either by the expansion of outputs along with the slack or can form a virtual DMU that can be formed by taking 86.67 per cent of the output of pcm, 3.9 per cent of Psy and 13.3 per cent of the output of tour. This virtual DMU can be formed without changing the input output ratio of the original DMU under evaluation. The weights in both the model shows that the second output that AM has 84 per cent share in increasing the efficiency score if AM increases by one unit and the third output NFD has been assigned zero weight. Hence, the expansion or contraction of that output does not have much value to the DMU. The scale of operation is projected to be CRS. That is the Virtual DMU will be operating under CRS and the DMU can expand its output at the present rate of input use and no need to change the ratio at which inputs are combined. The scale of operation, if CRS, then the DMU has no difficulty in expansion and contraction of the output at the existing input output combination.

While moving to the second case, it is observed that there is little impact of the merging of Math with Phy and Tour with Geog. The projection of outputs, output slacks and weighted output data do not show any drastic change.

However, the scale of operation has been change to DRS. This implies the fact that when the DMU is compared with the similar performing DMU on the basis of input output combination; its operation is showing some shortage of the fixed inputs. As a result the variable inputs are utilised to produce more output. Therefore, proportionate increase in the fixed inputs such as the area under the DMU, the faculty strength etc. are to be given more importance.

4.3.1.3. CCR and BCC model (third Case)

In the third case, five DMUs have been merged and both CCR and BCC model have been used to see the scale of operation at variable returns to scale technology. There is a vast change in the efficiency rank without change in the efficiency level. i.e., under CCR the rank is 9 and 13 under BCC model. The weights given to the output have not been changed. Hence, except the scale of operation, other things do not show any change. Therefore, the merging of these five DMUs has not shown any changes to the DMU even though there is overall change in the scenario.

4.3.2. International Relations (IR)

Table 4.8: The Details of the Results of IR under Three different cases

Items	*1st case*		*2nd case*		*3rd case*	
	CCR	*BCC*	*CCR*	*BCC*	*CCR*	*BCC*
Rank (score)	24(1.34)	23(1.149)	22(1.32)	23(1.31)	13(1.21)	15(1.128)
Reference Group	Pcm-86.67, Psy-3.93, Tour-13.32	Pcm-58.16, Hort-6.9, Geol-34.86	Pcm-69.35, Geol-37.6, Chin-9.7	Pcm-60.46, Geol-3.51, Phy-18.93, Chin-11.45, Antro-5.6	Pcm-52.01, Phy-21.14, Antro-16.27	Pcm-38.07, Phy-0, Antro-61.91
Inputs/ outputs	5,3, 27	5, 3, 27	5, 3, 25	5, 3, 25	5, 2, 22	5, 2, 22
Projection	34.28 each	14.93, 14.93, 37.17	32.64 each	31.08 each	21.73 each	12.87 each
Weight	16.01, 83.98,0	13.68, 86.31, 0(1.112)	52.94, 7.4, 39.59	36.32, 32.50, 32.16	15.56, 84.43	10.76, 89.23
RTS		DRS		DRS		CRS

4.3.2.1. CCR and BCC Model (first case)

The results of the efficiency analysis of IR are presented in Table 4.8. In all the three cases, the DMU is classified as relatively inefficient as the output efficiency score exceeds 1. In the 1st case the CCR score is 1.34 with a rank 24 and it increased to 23 in the BCC model. Under the CCR model, the DMU has the chance of increasing the output by 37 per cent without changing the output proportion. Since, there is no slack output; it does not have any kind of mix inefficiency. Thus, the DMU can increase the observed output from 286 to 384 (TRS), 57 to 76.5(AM) and 5 to 6.7(NFD) respectively.

The reference set of IR shows that it can achieve this increment without changing the ratio of output if it combines the output of PCM, Geol, Math and Chi in 73.79 per cent, 15.41 per cent, 27.24 per cent and 4.06 per cent respectively. The calculation of the projection is based on the reference group Lambda value. For example, The projected 1st output is

λ

$+\lambda$ λ value of PCM (actual 1st output of PCM)

$+\lambda$ $+\lambda$ value of Geol (observed 1st output of Geol)

$+\lambda$ $+\lambda$ value of Math (observed 1st output of Math)

$+\lambda$ value of Chi (observed 1st output of Chin)

=.7379(503)+.1541 ((58)+.27249(1)+.0406(89=(384).

The weighted output data () of IR shows 16 per cent weight is given to the 1st output and almost 84 per cent of the total weight is given to the 2nd output and the 3rd out with zero weight. It suggests that the DMU (IR) must focus on increasing the 1st and 2nd output which will help in increasing the efficiency rather than focusing on increasing the no. of first division students. More weighted output helps in reducing the inefficiency that is increasing the performance. Thus, creating more 1st division students in comparison to other two outputs definitely will not help in the performance improvement when all the DMUs are compared together.

The BCC model allows the DMU (IR) to be compared with the DMUs who are using similar technology (similar pattern of input-output combinations). The BCC score is 1.15 and ranked as 23rd DMU among the 27 DMUs. This score suggests that the DMU has the capability of improving the output by at least 15 per cent without increasing the inputs. The projections of outputs are 14 per cent, 14 per cent and 37 per cent respectively. The peer group has changed to pcm, Hort and Geol with a weight of 56.16 per cent, 6.9 per cent and 34.86 per cent respectively. It means PCM acted as a peer under both the situation. Inefficient DMU can be efficient if it produces the output at the above weights. The scale of operation is projected to be DRS as the peers are using either CRS or DRS technology. The projection of scale suggests that if its output to be expanded it will operate under the DRS. Hence, there will be limitation of the expansion in scale at higher level of output without increasing the size. The future planning should be focused more on the expansion of the basic infrastructure (Class-room, are, faculties and research facilities). The DMU is having both technical inefficiency and output slacks. So it is mix inefficient. The projection of 3rd output is

(BCC efficiency score* the observed 3rd output) + the slack of the 3rd output= 1.1492*5+1.1123=6.85 which is 37 per cent more than the observed 3rd output. Hence in order to be efficient the 1st two outputs are to be radially expanded by 14.93% and the 3rd output by 37 per cent.

4.3.2.2. CCR and BCC Model (Second Case)

In 2nd case when the total DMU decreased to 25 due to merging of Math with Phy and Tour with Geog, the rank improved to 22 with a score 1.32 under CCR but did not change under the BCC model. The output projection, weighted output data did not show any big differences which has to be noted seriously. The scale of operation also did not change. Hence, the Merging of small DMUs do not affect the performance of

IR. This conveys the message that IR does have any kind of similarity of operation with the math and Tour.

4.3.2.3. CCR and BCC Model (Third Case)

Under the 3rd case, CCR result shows that out of 22 DMUs the rank of IR has been improved to 13 with a score 1.21. This suggests that the DMU can improve its output by 21 per cent without any increment of inputs. The peer group weight suggests that 52 per cent of pcm, 21.14 per cent of phy and 16.27 per cent antro can produce the output that will lie on the frontier. Since there are no output slacks the inefficiency is purely on account of technical inefficiency and 22 per cent of radial expansion of each output can bring it onto the frontier. In other words, it can increase AM from 57 to 69 and TRS from 286 to 348. The contribution of AM to efficiency improvement is 84 per cent and the rest is by the1st output. This means the DMU should focus more on the TRS to improve its operation efficiently and effectively. The BCC model the efficiency has improved but the rank has been reduced to 15. It means when compared to similar DMUs its operation improved but relatively its improvement is less than the improvement of other similar DMUs. The major change is that under the BCC model the DMU is operating under the CRS indicating the radial expansion of output could be possible if the DMU is expanding its operation under the existing technology.

4.3.3. Political Science (Psc)

4.3.3.1. CCR and BCC Model (First Case)

Political Science (Psc), one of the important departments under the School of Social Sciences of Sikkim University. In case of CCR model (1st case) the DMU has been ranked at the last (27) with a score of 1.933. This means the DMU has the potential to increase the present level of outputs by 93 per cent more. The inefficiency is due to both technical inefficiency and radial inefficiency. This is possible if the DMU makes a virtual DMU consisting of Pcm, Hind, Psy and

Tour with a weight of 71 per cent, 41 per cent, 8.2 per cent and 51.2 per cent respectively. The output projection shows that it can radially expand the output (1st and 2nd) by 93 per cent and the 3rd output by almost 340 per cent. The addition of the slack of the 3rd output is around 1 unit.

Table 4.9: The Details of the Results of PSC under Three Different Cases

Items	*1st case*		*2nd case*		*3rd case*	
	CCR	*BCC*	*CCR*	*BCC*	*CCR*	*BCC*
Rank (score)	27 (1.933)	27 (1.258)	25(1.89)	25(1.45)	18(1.53)	11(1.026)
Reference Group	Pcm-.712, hind-.412, psy-.0826, tour-.512	Hort-.0207, micb-.4224, geol-.5568	Pcm-.5984, hind-1.048,	Pcm-.3417, geog-.2639, psy-.3942	Pcm-.3961, hind-.5372, psy-.083, edu-1.089	Micb-.2627, hind-.3469, mang-.3910
Inputs/ outputs	5, 3, 27	5, 3, 27	5, 3, 25	5,3, 25	5, 2, 22	5, 2, 22
Projection (slacks)	93, 93, 340, (.892)	25.85, 25.85, 250.87(6.15)	89, 89, 294(6.15)	45, 45, 218 (5.16)	53, 53	2.65, 2.65
Weight	.00023, .0173, 0	.00036, .0168, 0	.0622, .937	.08, .92	.0112, .99	34, 65
RTS	-	DRS		DRS		DRS

While choosing the expansion of output it gives more weight to the 2nd output than the 1st output and the 3rd output is given no weight (Table 4.9). However, under the BCC model the efficiency score increased to 1.258 but without any change in the ranking. The weights, projection rate remained almost same but the peers for the BCC model changed to Hort, micb and Geol with weights of 2 per cent, 42 per cent and 55 per cent respectively. The projection of scale efficiency is DRS. This suggests that the expansion of output in order to attain frontier output, leads to DRS. Thus, management of the efficient use of inputs could lead to a better performance of the DMU.

4.3.3.2. CCR and BCC Model (Second and third case)

The position of the DMU (both ranking and score) does not show any significant changes under the 2nd condition. Still its position remained at the lowest level of efficiency score. However, there is one significant change in the peers group in the two models. In case of CCR PCM and Hind were the peers but in case of BCC the set included PCM, Geog and Psy.

In third case, brings a phenomenal change in the two models. Under CCR model the rank increased to 18 with a score of 1.53 and in BCC case the rank further increased to 11 with a score of 1.026. It means under the situation of merging the DMU gets affected and becomes better than the previous case. In comparison to the case 1st and 2nd in 3rd case, the DMU has to increase only 2 per cent. So merging of the Law with Geog has a better impact and it would be a welcome step in merging the Law with PSc. The performance of the DMU increases as all the inputs are better utilised with the existing resources and there would be better management of the DMU.

4.3.4. Sociology (Soc)

4.3.4.1. CCR and BCC Model (First Case)

This DMU, Soc comes under the school of social sciences. In all the cases under all the models, the DMU is ranked inefficient with a rank that varies from 16-25. In the 1st case the CCR score is 1.27 and BCC score is 1.15. It means at a global comparison the DMU has to increase the output at least by 27 per cent but compared to the local environment it could come on to the frontier by increasing only 15 per cent of the present output. Among the CCR reference group it gives more weight to edu and hind and the lowest weight is given to pcm. In BCC case almost 90 per cent of the weight is given to edu. It implies the fact that soc can improve its position if it could combine the peers output as per the weights (lambda value) to become fully efficient.

4.3.4.2. CCR and BCC Model (Second and Third Case)

In the 2nd case the DMU efficiency has been improved

but the rank has been slipped to 22 from 20. That means the comparative performance of other similar DMU is better than the performance of Soc. However, the scale of operation was CRS in 1st case and it became DRS in the 2nd case. It means there are some peers who are operating under the DRS as well as CRS. Hence the projection of output to the frontier output will lead to DRS. Thus, the present operation at the existing input output rate follows DRS meaning that the DMU either lacks the fixed inputs in proportion to the variable input or there is ineffective managerial problem of the DMU. The effective management policy in the present scale of operation might help improving the situation in the long run.

Table 4.10: The Details of the Results of SOC under Three different cases

Items	*1st case*		*2nd case*		*3rd case*	
	CCR	*BCC*	*CCR*	*BCC*	*CCR*	*BCC*
Rank (score)	22(1.27)	25(1.15)	20(1.27)	22(1.192)	16(1.44)	16(1.158)
Reference Group	Law-22.09, pcm-13.34, hind-24.17, edu-55.80	Pcm-.085, psy-.017, edu-.898	Law-.22, pcm-.133, Hind-.241, edu-.558	Pcm-.092, chin,.197, hind-.052, geog-.062, edu-.5953	Pcm-.2212, hind-.4785, psy-.1406	Pcm-.085, hind-.03, psy-.0214, edu-.8931
Inputs/ outputs	5,3 27	5,3, 27	5, 3, 25	5, 3, 25	5,2, 22	5, 2, 22
Projection	27.18, 27.18, 27.18	15.88, 15.88, 55.37	27.18, 27.18, 27, 18	19.3, 19.3, 19.3	44.05, 44.05, 44.05	15.87, 15.87, 15.87
Weighted data	20.80, 51.34, 27.85	6.5, 93.42, 0 (5.134)	20.80, 51.34, 27.85	10.57, 81.13, 8.29	4.85, 95.41,	6.6, 93.4
RTS		CRS		DRS		CRS

In the 3rd case (under the scenario of merging) the CCR score become 1.44 (rank 16) but the BCC score improved to 1.158 (rank 16). That is under the CRS technology, the DMU could further expand its output by almost 44 per cent. The inefficiency is purely on account of technical inefficiency. The weighted data suggests that DMU the 2nd output is given around 95 per cent share in the increment of the efficiency score if the output increases by one unit and the 1st output is given only 5 per cent weights. Therefore, it should be commented that the present condition gives more importance to AM of the students rather than on TRS. Under the 3rd situation the DMU is projected to be operating under the CRS technology. Hence, the DMU can expand the output to a larger scale if this present input output structure is followed. Therefore, merging of the DMU has a favourable impact on the DMU in its scale of operation.

4.3.5. Botany (Bot)

4.3.5.1. CCR and BCC Model (First Case)

The details of the CCR and BCC scores and Ranks under three different situations are presented in Table 4.11. Botany (Bot) comes under the school of Physical sciences. In the 1st case out of 27 DMUs Bot is ranked 18 with a score of 1.07 and under BCC the rank reduced to 19 but the score improved to 1.006. In the 1st case it shows that the DMU can be fully efficient by increasing the output by 7 per cent only where as in the 2nd case the DMU is just slightly below the fully efficient frontier. The existing output structure shows that the expansion of the 1st and 2nd output does not add to reduction in the cost and the 3rd output has been assigned 100 per cent weight.

Table 4.11: The Details of the Results of Bot under Three different cases

Items	*1st case*		*2nd case*		*3rd case*	
	CCR	*BCC*	*CCR*	*BCC*	*CCR*	*BCC*
Rank (score)	18(1.07)	19(1.006)	17(1.07)	1891.02)	17(1.49)	20(1.42)
Reference Group	Geog-29.1, antro-5.7, mang-43.45, masc-34.47	Hort-27.61, geol-44.11, psy-1.57, edu-24.03, masc-2.66	Hort-3.94, geol-28.58, antro-4.18, mang-42.96, masc-29.4	Geol-24.55, psy-5.38, antro-9.01, edu-21.17, mang-19.76, masc-20.12	Zool-32.67, hist-35.29, antro-56.86	Zool-16.34, hist-53.59, antro-30.06
Inputs/ outputs	5,3,27	5, 3 27	5, 3, 25	5,3, 25	5, 2, 22	5, 2, 22
Projection	7.14, 10.37, 7.14	2.22, 93.29, 4.49	0, 0, 1	1.47, 63.79, 34.81	0(32.93), 1,	4.86, 95.14
Weight	0, 0 (.325,) 1	68, 68, 68	7.14, 7.14, 7.14	2.17, 2.17, 2.17	17.79, 49.39	42.12, 42.12
RTS		DRS		DRS		CRS

This phenomena shows that the DMU could able to perform better only because of large number of the students scoring 1st divisions. The slack figure of the 2nd output suggests increasing the output by 2 units does not affect the efficiency score. Therefore, when is compared to all the DMUs with different pattern of production it remains inefficient in other aspects. Among all the peers in CCR model, Mang is assigned highest weight (43.45 per cent) followed by Masc (34.47 per cent) but under BCC model the peers group and weights changed completely. Geol was chosen with highest weight (44 per cent) followed by Hort (27.61 per cent).

4.3.5.2. CCR and BCC Model (Second and Third Case)

The 2nd case does not show any kind of spectacular change due to merging of two DMUs. The 3rd situation also did not bring any change in the performance of the DMU. Therefore, Bot is not sensitive to changes in the number of DMU to be compared and the number of outputs to be produced. This shows that the inefficiency does not arise due to scale inefficiency rather purely technical inefficiency leads to the inefficiency and this can be corrected through better managerial practice of utilising the inputs in a most efficient manner.

Table 4.12: The Details of the Results of CHE under Three different cases

Items	*1st case*		*2nd case*		*3rd case*	
	CCR	*BCC*	*CCR*	*BCC*	*CCR*	*BCC*
Rank (score)	23(1.30)	20(1.06)	21(1.28)	21(1.131)	12(1.21)	1(1)
Reference Group	Pcm-2.96, zool-28.85, math-10.21, hind-76.25, edu-10.53	Hort-27.61, geol-44.11, psy-1.57, edu-24.03, masc-2.66	Pcm-6.3, zool-37.82, hind-79.88, edu-8.2	Zool-32.57, phy-11.89, hist-47.57, edu-7.9	Zool-1.95, hind-24.52	
Inputs/ outputs	5, 3, 27	5, 3, 27	5, 3, 25	5, 3, 25	5, 2, 22	5, 2, 22
Projection	30.02 each	10.38, 6.48, 6.48	28.20 each	18.97, 13.14, 13.14	63.67, 21.58	
Weighted data	11.37, 22.57, 66.05	0(3.89), 99.79, 0.02	9.5, 22.8, 66.6	0, 87.37, 12.62	0 (66.49), 1,	0, 1
RTS		DRS		DRS		DRS

4.3.6. Chemistry (Chem)

Chemistry (Chem) comes under the school of Physical Sciences. This is one of the few DMUs who could change its position from inefficiency to efficient state under the merger. In 1st case and 2nd case there is no such significant changes in scores and ranking but in the 3rd case the score improved to 1 under the BCC model. The CCR score is 1.21 and ranked 12 out of 22 DMUs. The peers are Zool and Hind with a weight of 2 per cent and 24 per cent respectively. The output projection under 3rd case shows that it could increase the 1st output by 64 per cent and the 2nd output by 22 per cent respectively. Whereas, the weighted data shows the contribution to the 1st input to the output efficiency score is zero. Since its marginal cost is zero it can improve this output by 66 points without changing the efficiency score. The projection of scale efficiency is DRS. This suggests that the DMU rate of output expansion is less than the rate of increase in the inputs.

4.3.7. Physics (Phy)

The results of CCR and BCC model in all the three cases are reported in the Table 4.13. This department (Phy) is the only DMU who changed its inefficient position to fully efficient position in all the three cases except the CCR model of the 1st case. In the CCR model of 1st case. It scored 1.07 with a rank 19 out of 27. It s peer group consists of Math (77%), Pcm (50.42%) and Geol (14%). The model projected that the inefficiency is due to both technical inefficiency and inefficiency due to output shortage. The output projection suggests that it is capable of increasing the three outputs by 7 per cent 49 per cent and 7 per cent respectively. The weighted data suggests that the total reduction of cost due to increase in the 2nd output is zero. That means it does not add anything to the efficient performance of the DMU. Therefore it has the flexibility of increasing the 2nd output in order to increase the output equivalent to the efficient DMU.

In all other cases, the DMU becomes fully efficient. Hence it can be suggested that this DMU could perform efficiently under the local environment and its efficiency score remains at 1 when there is merging of tour with it and other merging as well. The scale efficiency suggests that its projection of scale is CRS. It can expand the output radially without any change in the output ratio.

Table 4.13: The Details of the Results of Phy under Three Different Cases

Items	*1st case*		*2nd case*		*3rd case*	
	CCR	*BCC*	*CCR*	*BCC*	*CCR*	*BCC*
Rank (score)	19(1.07)	1	1	1	1	1
Reference Group	Pcm-50.42, geol-14.59, math-77.25					
Inputs/ Outputs	5, 3, 27					
Projection	7.30, 49.59, 7.30					
Weighted data	36.3,0 (26.22), 63.69					
RTS		DRS		CRS		CRS

4.3.8.1. CCR and BCC Model (First, Second and Third case)

The 1st department under the school of language is English (eng). The CCR and BCC results in all the three situations are given in the Table-4.14. The DMU remained inefficient in all the situations applied to CCR and BCC model. The inefficiency is ascribed purely to technical inefficiency. Unlike phy and chem. This DMU did not get any benefit of the merger of Chin with this. The DMU did not show any differences in the score as well as ranking in the 1st two situations. Its rank remained at 24 and 25. The CCR score suggests that there is possibility of 61 per cent of increase in the present output without any cost added to the production. This is only when all the 27 DMU are compared together. But Under BCC the score indicated possibility of increase in

21 per cent of the existing output without any additional cost. The reference group in the CCR model in all the 3 situations remained unaltered. The weighted output data shows that the 2nd output adds 85 per cent of the total benefit accrued to the DMU. Among all the peers psy has been given highest weight (60 per cent)

In the 3rd case, the CCR score improved from 1.61 to 1.49 but the rank slipped from 20 to 21. This means the improvement of performance under variable returns to scale is comparatively less in case of eng compared to the other similar DMUs who are using similar technology. The CRS projection indicates that the DMU can expand or contract its operation with the existing output ratio. Under the BCC model, the Virtual efficient DMU that can produce output at efficient level consists of pcm (36 per cent), hind (29 per cent) and psy (34 per cent). Under BCC model both the outputs have been assigned equal weights. Hence, the merger of Chin with English can improve its efficiency and ranks and it would be a good step in doing so.

Table 4.14: The Details of the Results of Eng under Three different cases

Items	*1st case*		*2nd case*		*3rd case*	
	CCR	*BCC*	*CCR*	*BCC*	*CCR*	*BCC*
Rank (score)	25(1.61)	26(1.21)	24(1.6)	24(1.31)	20(1.61)	21(1.49)
Reference Group	Pcm-39.22, psy-67.72, edu-19.97, tour-10.79	Hort-1.37, Micb-29.78,geol-26.18, psy-42.66	Pcm-36.8, hind-19.66, psy-60.18, edu-20.05	Pcm-12.84, micb-9.27, nep-4.84, geol-12.86, psy-60.11	Pcm-38.71, psy-92.18, edu-4.65	Pcm-36.15, hind-29.80, psy-34.03
Inputs/ outputs	5, 3, 27	5, 3, 27	5, 3, 25	5, 3, 25	5, 2, 22	5, 2, 22
Projection	61.74 each	21.89, 21.89, 23.72	60.94 each	31.25,	61.31, 61.31	41.48 each
Weighted data	9.69, 85.34, 4.97	6.3, 93.6, 0 (.1275)	6.2, 91.25, 2.48	19.49, 71.90, 8.6	12.75, 87.24	47.48, 52.51
RTS		DRS		DRS		CRS

4.3.9. Geography(geog)

4.3.9.1. *CCR and BCC Model (1*st, *2*nd *and 3*rd *Case)*

Like phy Geography department (geog) has got the befit of merger of tour with geog.. when there was no merging the CCR score was 1.80 with a rank of 26 that means it was the 2nd last inefficient DMU and its peer set consisted of pcm, zool, antro and edu with the lambda value of 103 per cent, 35.29 per cent, 14.56 per cent and 41.72 per cent respectively. It has both technical and slack inefficiency, hence called weakly efficient. Under the BCC model the efficiency score improved to 1.151 suggesting only 15 per cent improvement in the output could lead to full efficiency. The RTS is projected to be DRS indicating 3rd stage of production where the DMU has declining marginal product of the input may be due to excess of the variable inputs used. The output projection suggests that the 3rd output has a slack and it could expand its quantity without changing the efficiency score.

In the 2nd situation, the DMU's performance has improved amazingly under the BCC model. It could become fully efficient under BCC model. The CCR model does not show any change from the 1st situation.

Table 4.15: The Details of the Results of Geog under Three different cases

Items	*1st case*		*2nd case*		*3rd case*	
	CCR	*BCC*	*CCR*	*BCC*	*CCR*	*BCC*
Rank (score)	26(1.80)	24(1.15)	23(1.50)	1	22(2.23)	18(1.33)
Reference Group	Pcm-1.03, zool-35.29, antr-14.56, edu-41.72	Hort-39.26, micb-60.73	Pcm-61.22, hind-126, edu-87.72		Pcm-154, hind-33	Micb-80.8, hind-2.14, mang-17.02
Inputs/ outputs	5, 3, 27	5, 3, 27	5, 3, 25	5, 3, 25	5, 2, 22	5, 2, 22
Projection	80.16, 113.52, 80.16	15.13, 15.13, 25.75	50.64 each		133.22 each	33.24 each
Weight	31.04,0 (19.67), 68.53	16.57, 83.42,0 (1.05)	25.87, 47.25, 26.87		39.22 (66.49), 60.77	55.14, 44.85
RTS		DRS		DRS		DRS

The most distinguishing feature of this DMU is that the position of ranking and score did not show any remarkable changes when other mergers are allowed. Therefore, the Merger of Tour with Geog would be technically a correct step in enhancing the performance of geog.

4.3.10. Commerce (Comm)

4.3.10.1. CCR and BCC Model (first case)

Table 4.16 reports the results of CCR and BCC model under the three different situations.

This is the only DMU which does not show any kind of sensitivity in efficiency score and rankings when two DMUs are allowed to merge with some of the related DMUs. The ranking remained stable either at 19 to 22. But unfortunately it got affected badly when five DMU are merged. The efficiency score under CCR model shows that 84 per cent of the output could be increased without any additional cost to the production. This remains same under BCC model also. The CRS projection strongly indicates the expansion of the output without any change in the existing ratio could be done easily. Hence, the better input management could lead to better performance.

Table 4.16: The Details of the Results of Comm under Three Different cases

Items	*1st case*		*2nd case*		*3rd case*	
	CCR	*BCC*	*CCR*	*BCC*	*CCR*	*BCC*
Rank (score)	21(1.24)	22(1.107)	19(1.24)	20(1.07)	21(1.84)	22(1.83)
Reference Group	Geol-103.2, edu-55.01	Geol-17.2, edu-2.24, mang-80.53	Geol-103, edu-55.01	Geol-17.2, edu-2.24, mang-80.53	Hind-64, psy-1.51, edu-43	Hin-77.87, psy-23.34, edu-3.7
Inputs/ outputs	5,3, 27	5,3, 27	5,35 27	5,3,25	5,2, 22	5,2, 22
Projection	72.59, 81.10,24.6	89.89, 13.22, 10.74	72.59, 81.10, 24.60	89.89, 13.22, 10.74	122.87, 84.11	99.84, 83.22
Weighted data	37..92, 35.59, 0	62.53, 1.56, 0	37.91, 35.59, 0	62.53, 1.56	30.61, 0	13.13, 0
RTS		CRS		CRS		CRS

As outlined above, the efficiency evaluation of the DMUs have been carried out using the DEA analysis especially using the CCR and BCC method with output orientation under three different situations. In the first case, all the 27 DMUs the CCR mean score was 0.91 and 17 DMUs were under ranked as CCR efficient (score=1). However, all the CCR-efficient DMUs have been assigned the rank of 1. Hence, it would be rather difficult to know which DMU among the fully efficient DMUs is better one. In order to have unique ranking of the CCR efficient DMUs, the Super Efficiency (SE) model is used. This model will rank all the fully efficient DMUs without changing the CCR efficiency score of the relatively inefficient DMUs. It means the SE method compares the DMUs whose CCR score is 1.

As we know, the inefficient DMUs adopt some of or all of the fully efficient DMUs as their Peers in producing the output on the frontier level. As far as the frequency of Peers is concerned, PCM is used to be the maximum number of times peers (8) for the inefficient DMUs followed by Edu (5) and Geol (4 times). Among the Peers Hist, Nep, Micb are not considered as peers by any of the inefficient DMUs. Similarly, Chin and Law DMUs acted as peers for one DMU only. These DMUs (score=1) are considered to be CCR efficient because they neither have any input surpluses or output shortages. Therefore, those DMUs whose input output slacks are zero and the efficiency score is 1, they are called strongly efficient or *Pareto Koopman efficient* DMU.

As far as the weighted data are concerned, Geol, Math, Hind, Psy, Tour more emphasis on teaching and the AM. It implies that the DMUs have of course attained efficiency, the output weight indicates that larger weight is given to AM neglecting TRS. Therefore, these DMUs who give maximum weight on any one output become relatively more efficient than other DMUs. But the efficiency evaluation under the BCC model shown increase in the number of fully efficient

DMUs from 17 to 18. Phy become efficient under the BCC technology. So 17 DMUs, except Phy, are considered to be the MPSS DMUs. It is projected to be operating under DRS. It means further expansion of output by increasing input will lead to declining marginal return of these inputs and output rate will decline.. The DRS is in operation due to the fact that the DMU has some shortage of the fixed inputs like lab facilities in comparison to the demand of the faculties and students. Excess of the variable inputs in comparison to the fixed inputs leads to excess utilisation of the capacity beyond optimum level. Therefore, the supply of the fixed assets like lab equipments, scientific infrastructure should be given top priority in improving the scale of operation.

4.3.10.2. CCR and BCC Model (Second and Third Case)

In the 2nd case the merging of Tour with Geog and Math with Phy does not affect the efficiency scores but the ranking and Geog become efficient under BCC. It means merging Tour with Geog has an advantage of improving the scale of operation and projected to be operating under DRS.

This suggests that the shortage of the fixed inputs (faculties, Laboratory, sufficient class-rooms, faculty rooms) is the main constraints and its expansion is to be given more importance rather than increasing the number of students admitted into the course.

But in the 3rd case, when five small DMUs have been merged with other DMUs, then it has large consequences on the CCR efficiency scores and the ranking. The CCR score reduced to 82 per cent and the BCC score reduced to .89 in comparison to the 1st and 2nd case. Under the three cases, the DMUs operating under MPSS are Edu, Psy, Antro, PCM, Hind, Phy and Zool as their efficiency score remains stable under different scale of operation and different environment. The most significant implication of these MPSS is that the input output structure is such that these DMUs can adhere to any condition under any type of technology (input=output relation) and hence, they are preferred as the most frequent peers.

4.4. Super Efficiency Model (SE)

The DEA model introduced by Charnes *et. al.,* (1978) is used for estimating the relative efficiency of a set of homogeneous DMUs with multiple inputs and multiple output of the two groups: fully efficient and relatively inefficient. The fully efficient DMU cannot be ranked because of the unit scores of all such DMUs. Pioneered by Banker and Gifford ( ) and Banker *et. al.,* ( ) the Super Efficiency (SE) implies the possible chance of a DMU in expanding the inputs or contracting the output without becoming inefficient. Hence, SE is an important measurement to rank the extremely efficient DMUs.

Anderson and Peterson (AP) introduced SE as a ranking methodology to differentiate the performance of extreme efficient DMUs. However, this model (both CRS and VRS) has a crucial issue of infeasibility. The infeasibility occurs when an efficient DMUs under evaluation cannot come to the frontier formed by the rest of the DMUs via increasing the inputs or decreasing the outputs depending on the type of orientation.

Three types of models: Super radial output oriented model, Super SBM output oriented model and the super SBM non-oriented model (all with CRS assumption) are used for all the alternatives cases (without merging and with merging) are used to evaluate the ranking of the fully efficient DMU. Table 4.17 shows the rankings and scores of all the efficient DMUs under Super Efficiency Models

Table 4.17: Rankings and Scores of the fully efficient DMUs under Three Alternative Models (1st Case)

DMUs	***Scores (Ranks) Radial***	***DMUs***	***Scores (Ranks) SBM***	***DMU***	***Scores (Ranks) SBM non-oriented***
Psy	0(1)	Psy	1.17E+16 (1)	Chin	1.369104(1)
Chin	3.555934(2)	PCM	1.3819095(2)	PCM	1.302881(2)
PCM	2.067925(3)	Chin	1.3782202(3)	Law	1.266575(3)
Law	1.691991(4)	Law	1.3516328(4)	Math	1.193518(4)
Edu	1.578085(5)	Math	1.3059314(5)	Geol	1.174421(5)
Math	1.571684(6)	Antro	1.2572263(6)	Edu	1.160355(6)
Geol	1.449704(7)	Geol	1.2307048(7)	Antro	1.151985 (7)
Nep	1.322995(8)	Edu	1.1603549(8)	Hind	1.080537(8)
Antro	1.287942(9)	Nep	1.1535047(9)	Nep	1.0727(9)
Hind	1.226284(10)	Hind	1.0843546(10)	Masc	1.047867(10)
Tour	1.1312(11)	Zool	1.0550546 (11)	Zool	1.044895(11)
Masc	1.102182(12)	Masc	1.0478669 (12)	Tour	1.036624(12)
Zool	1.093296(13)	Tour	1.0425257(13)	His	1.01222(13)
Mang	1.034125(14)	Micb	1.0134018(14)	Mang	1.011484(14)
Hist	1.030837(15)	His	1.0127352(15)	Micb	1.008461(15)
Micb	1.020902(16)	Mang	1.0115164(16)	Psy	1.003686(16)
Hort	1(17)				

Table 4.17 shows the scores and ranking of the Super radial model in 2nd column, the scores and ranks of SBM model in column 4 and last column the scores and ranks of the SBM non-oriented model has been reported. Out of the 27 DMUs 17 DMUs were fully efficient and as per the super Radial model, Psy is ranked 1 and Hort is ranked as the last DMU of the fully efficient DMUs. As per the output projection, it can be said that Chin can remain efficient if it reduces the 1st and 2nd output by 71.88 per cent and the 3rd output by 95 per cent. It means the reduction of output still does not affect efficiency score. Hence, the DMU which has the largest possibility of reducing the output to reach at the frontier is ranked as the super efficient DMU and ranked as 1.

The alternative models have been tried to avoid the infeasibility problem. As seen from column 4 and 6 of Table 4.17, the rank of Geol, Hind, Masc and Hist remained with the same rank under SBM model. However, under the SBM non-oriented model, except Psy Antro, Micb all other DMUs shown improvement in the ranking.

Table 4.18: Rankings and Scores of the fully efficient DMUs under Three Alternative Models (2nd Case)

DMU	*Score (Rank) Radial*	*DMU*	*Score (Rank) SBM*	*DMU*	*Score (Rank) SBM non-oriented*
Psy	0	Psy	5.29E+15	Chin	1.369104
Chin	3.555934	PCM	1.3819095	PCM	1.302881
PCM	2.067925	Chin	1.3782202	Law	1.266575
Law	1.691991	Law	1.3516328	Geol	1.174421
Edu	1.580881	Antro	1.2572263	Edu	1.160996
Geol	1.532688	Geol	1.2327491	Antro	1.151985
Nep	1.322995	Edu	1.1609955	Hind	1.080537
Antro	1.287942	Nep	1.1535047	Nep	1.0727
Hind	1.22814	Hind	1.0843546	Masc	1.047867
Masc	1.102182	Zool	1.0550546	Zool	1.044895
Zool	1.093296	Masc	1.0478669	His	1.01222
Mang	1.034125	Micb	1.0134018	Mang	1.011484
His	1.030837	His	1.0127352	Micb	1.008461
Micb	1.020902	Mang	1.0115164	Phy	1.005802
Phy	1.018339	Phy	1.0071132	Psy	1.003686
Hort	1				

The Super efficiency scores of the three models under the 2nd case is reported in Table 4.18. Out of 25 DMUs 16 DMUs were efficient and their rankings are reported in column 2, 4 and 6. Psy is ranked 1st and His ranked the last among the fully efficient DMUs. In SBM model psy ranked 1st and Phy ranked last. But in case of Non-oriented model Chin was ranked 1st and Psy is ranked last.

Table 4.19: Rankings and Scores of the fully efficient DMUs under Three Alternative Models (3rd Case)

DMU	*Score (Rank) Radial*	*DMU*	*Score (rank) SBM*	*DMU*	*Score (Rank) Non-Oriented*
Psy	2.689394	Psy	1.954459	PCM	1.530521
PCM	2.067925	PCM	1.723058	Psy	1.364958
Hind	1.420697	Hind	1.183815	Hind	1.183086
Phy	1.283582	Antro	1.171195	Antro	1.083091
Antro	1.262324	Phy	1.124183	Phy	1.057436
Zool	1.124943	Zool	1.058798	Zool	1.032461
Edu	1.023642	Edu	1.011793	Edu	1.0056

The super efficiency results of the three models in 3rd case are reported in Table 4.19. The number of fully efficient DMU reduced to Seven. Out of which Psy and Edu ranked 1st and last respectively under the Super Radial Model. When SBM is applied Antro's rank increased from 5 to 4. Rank of Psy, PCM, Hind and Edu remained intact. In case of Non-Oriented SBM model, PCM ranked 1 and Psy ranked 2 but Antro and Phy interchanged their rank as compared to the SBM model.

Now if the ranks of the DMUs are compared in the 3rd case then Psy, PCM and Hind ranked at the top in descending order and Edu remained at the last ranking.

In the 2nd case, Chin, PCM and law secured 2nd, 3rd and 4th position respectively and in 1st case Chin, PCM and Law ranked at the top with descending order. Hence, in all the three cases PCM and Chin have been ranked at the top.

4.5. Conclusion

In order to study the present structure and functioning of individual department, to calculate the relative efficiency of each department, the input-output slacks, the peer groups of the inefficient departments, projection of input mix/output mix that the department can reduce/ increase without affecting the current level of output, the study undertakes an empirical analysis of the efficiency evaluation of all the departments (27) of Sikkim University. The study has used two models of DEA such as CCR, BCC to compute the efficiency and rankings of each department (using five inputs and producing three outputs) under three different situations: (1) when all the departments are considered with all inputs and all outputs; (2) when two departments such as Math and Tour are merged with Phy and Geog using the same inputs and output; (3) five departments have been merged to see the changes in the rankings and efficiency scores of the departments. Lastly, Super efficiency model has been utilised (Radial, SBM output oriented and non-oriented model) to rank the fully efficient DMUs since all the fully efficient DMUs under CCR model are assigned the value 1.

Owing to the comparative superiority of output oriented approach, the CCR and BCC models with output orientation have been employed to all three cases. As far as the 1st case is concerned, as per the CCR model, out of 27 DMUs, 17 DMUs are found to be fully efficient (tour, hist, mang, law, pcm, edu, psy, antro, hort, micb, zool, nep, geol, math, hind, and chin) and the inefficient DMUs are bot, phy, eco, comm., soc, chem, IR, eng, geog, and psc. Among them three DMUs (bot, phy and eco are in the range of 90 per cent and above; one DMU (comm.) in the range of 80 per cent and 89 per cent; three DMUs (soc, chem. and IR) in the range of 70 per cent to 79 per cent and three DMUs between 50 per cent and 69 per cent (eng, geog and psc). Psc got the lowest ranking among all the 27 DMUs.

The CCR Mean efficiency score suggests that on an average the efficiency can increase by reducing the inputs by 10 three without changing the level of output. As far as the peers are concerned, pcm is acted as the most favourable peer (eight times) followed by edu (five times) and geog (four times). However, under the BCC model the average efficiency score (BCC score) increased to 0.96 indicating improvement of operation under variable returns to scale. The number of DMUs operated efficiently increased from 17 to 18. The DMU which operated under full efficiency (hist, law, pcm, hort, micb, zool, geol, math, phy, chin, hind, nep, antro, psy, edu, mang, masc and tour). Masc improved its operation and reached to full efficiency. Under BCC model, psy, antro, edu, hort and geol are considered as the maximum number of times (five times) peers for inefficient DMUs.

As far as the scale of operation is concerned, 17 DMUs were fully efficient. Hence, they are operating under CRS and three DMUs (eco, soc and comm.) are projected to operate under CRS.

However, one fully BCC efficient DMU, phy is operating under DRS and DMUs are projected to be operating under DRS such as (IR, Psc, Bot, Chem., Eng and Geog). Hence, 17 DMUs are considered to be most Productive Scale and Size. These DMUs have the characteristics of radial expansion and contraction without any proportionate change in input-output ratio.

In case of CCR model (1st case) the share of contribution of 2nd output (AM) is much higher to the improvement in efficiency followed by the 1st output (TRS). For eco, psc, eng and comm., production of 2nd output have largest share (more than 80 per cent) in the efficiency score.

While moving to the 2nd case, out of 25 DMUs, 15 DMU become fully efficient and 10 DMUs remain less efficient. The mean efficiency score is 0.911 with a SD of 0.13. PCM acted as the most frequently referred DMU (seven times) followed by Hind and Edu (six and five times respectively) for the inefficient DMUs. The fully efficient DMUs are (masc, mang, hist, edu, law, pcm, psy, antro, nep, hort, micb, hind, geol, phy and chin) and the inefficient DMUs are (bot, eco, comm., soc, chem., IR, geog, eng and psc). The mean efficiency of the inefficient DMUs is 0.75 i.e., there is chance of 25 per cent improvement on an average of all inefficient DMUs.

Due to merging of tour with geog, it become fully efficient and similarly phy became fully efficient. Under BCC model, the mean efficiency score improved to 0.94 with a minimum score of 0.68. The number of fully efficient DMUs 17 and inefficient DMUs are eight. There is no change in positions of other DMUs. The only change under this situation is that merging made these two DMUs fully efficient without having any bad consequences for other DMUs.

The returns to scale indicate that 16 DMUs who are both CCR and BCC efficient are operating under CRS and comm is projected to be operating under CRS. One BCC efficient DMU (geog) is operating under DRS and other seven inefficient DMUs are projected to be operating under DRS. As realised from the observed input-output combination, some DMUs have very less number of outputs and inputs which will constrain the feasible region of operation. Hence, five DMUs (as discussed in the methodology) were allowed to merge with related DMUs (functional similarity). Out of all the outputs the NFD is dropped in this case. Under this situation the number of efficient DMUs reduced to seven and 15 DMUs could not achieve full efficiency. The mean efficiency (CCR) score is 0.818 which is less compared to earlier two cases. The fully efficient DMUs are (edu, psy, antro, hind, pcm, zool). After merging geol with Chem, math with phy, chin with eng, law with psc and tour with geog, except phy no other DMUs could achieve full efficiency. The mean efficiency of inefficient DMUs is calculated to be 0.734 i.e., they can improve their performance at least by 27 per cent. Under the situation, geog is ranked as the least performed DMU.

Under BCC model, the number of full efficient DMUs increased to 10 and 12 DMUs remained inefficient. The mean score is calculated to be 0.896 with a minimum score of 0.54. The most frequently chosen peer DMU is Hind (11 times) followed by pcm (seven times) and psy (six times). The fully BCC efficient DMUs are mang, edu, psy, antro, pcm, hind, phy, chem., zool, micb) still geog, eng remained inefficient whereas, the rank of geog improved to 18 and rank of eng reduced to 21. The least performed DMU is comm. with a score of 0.545.

Out of the ten fully efficient DMUs, seven are operating under CRS (pcm, hind, antro, psy, edu, phy, zool). The rest DMUs (chem., micb and mang) are projected to operate under DRS. The three efficient DMUs are projected to operate under DRS (psc, hort and geog). The other nine DMUs are projected to be operating under DRS. The implication is that those DMUs operating under CRS can either expand or contract the output without changing the input ratio.

But those operating under DRS, suggests that DMUs are shortage of some of inputs and huge excess of the variable inputs. So expansion of the fixed inputs in comparison to variable inputs could change the scale of operation.

The most interesting fact is that the no DMU is operating under IRS indicating the situation that no DMU has unutilised fixed inputs.

Further, the application of super efficiency model ranks the model fully efficient DMU. As per the three models, chin, pcm and law ranked as the top ranked DMUs (with a slight change in position) and hist, mang and micb remained at the lowest of the ranking of fully efficient DMU. It means these DMUs cannot reduce the output if they are to remain efficient. Hence, the entire analysis suggests that psy, pcm, hind, antro, zool and edu remained fully efficient in all the three situations. When math and tour are merged, it improved the efficiency of phy and geog to full efficiency without affecting other DMUs. But under the 3rd case, the merging has a bad impact even on the fully efficient DMUs. Except phy, no other DMU in which other DMUs are merged could achieve full efficiency. It means size of operation does not allow the merging to be beneficial except math and tour.

4.6. Suggestions

Based on the results of efficiency analysis of all the departments of Sikkim University, the following suggestions have been proposed for the improvement of inefficient DMUs.

1. As far as the inputs are considered, the area under the department has positive correlation with the number of permanent faculties. Therefore, both expansion of area and recruitment of permanent faculties are essentially required for departments who are inefficient and operating under diminishing returns to scale.
2. Lack of permanent faculties not only affects the teaching quality but also reduce the output on research activities. Hiring of ad hoc faculties only enhances the current expenditure without adding anything to the enhancement of efficiency. Therefore, huge investment on building, permanent infrastructure (class-rooms, laboratory, faculty rooms, departmental library, central library equipped with textbooks, referred books, back volumes of journals, current journals, data bases, computer lab with all modern facilities, rooms for M.Phil and PhD students.
3. Since, the university does not have permanent campus, the current expenditure has become huge irrespective of the size of the operation (number of students admitted into the course, number of courses launched and number of teachers engaged). The variable cost for maintenance remains almost same and it goes on increasing as the size is increasing above a certain level. Therefore, total expenditure of the small departments are not so small compared to the large departments. Hence, centralised structure for the university is an urgent need.
4. From the data, it is clear that social Sciences consisting of seven departments has no professor (2014-15) and only four associate professors. On an average, the

school of social sciences has only three faculties. The situation is worse in school of languages, Human Science and Professional Studies. Therefore, urgent attention must be given towards recruitment of faculties without considering the fact that financial constraints dominates over the issue.

5. As per the data, the girl students in almost all the departments perform better than the boys' in their respective courses. Therefore, more attention should be given for the improvement of the performances of boys in their courses. Since, the girls enrolment in Science subjects are less, efforts must initiated to make the science course attractive for the girls student. Further, the admission procedure for the girls' students in the science stream should be relaxed to an allowable limit for better enrolment of girls' students. Counselling of students and parents at the UG and PG level must be made to persuade the students into these streams.
6. As in some of the departments, the average marks of the students is less than or equal to 50 per cent, the nature of the subject calls for strict attendance of the students. Failing of strict attendance norms develop a casual behaviour on attending classes regularly. This might be one of the reasons for low performance of the male students. Second, the examination system should enforce prohibition of the students failing the attendance of the required percentage.
7. Compulsory crash courses should be given in technical subjects (eco, math, phy, chem) to the weak students who are unable to cope of with the course in the first semester itself.
8. The result suggests that the improvement of inefficient departments in the first case (CCR and BCC model) could be achieved by focusing more on TRS and AM. The faculties must allocate qualitative time for

teaching the courses. Strict enforcement of good quality teaching with high standard must be enforced seriously to improve the standard of teaching.

9. The merging of math and tour with phy and geog improves the position of the phy and geog efficiency without adversely affecting the rankings and scores of other departments. Therefore, merging of these two departments is strongly recommended to have overall improvement in the efficiency.
10. Further merger other departments such geol with Chem, math with phy, chin with eng, law with psc and tour with geog do not seem to be favourable for overall improvement of the departments. Rather, the number of departments operating under full efficiency reduced to seven and the number of inefficient departments increased to 15. Therefore, merger at large scale of the above departments is not suggested as the differences in the size of operation do not allow being beneficial.
11. In all the cases, psy, pcm, hind, antro, zool and edu remained peers for all other inefficient departments. These departments are considered as the most productive in scale and size. These departments can be considered as role models for others at the existing input-output structure.
12. On the basis of super efficiency ranking, chin, pcm and law remained as the top super efficient department with top ranks in all three cases and hist, mang and micb remained as the lowest ranked fully efficient departments.
13. Since no department under any case is operating under increasing returns to scale, the stage of operation of each department is not at primary level. As majority of departments are projected to be operating under DRS, policy should be focused on expansion of fixed assets as mentioned above.

4.7. Limitations of the Study

1. Since, the university is functioning without permanent campus, the efficiency evaluation is not a permanent indicator. It is limited to the particular year under the study.
2. As the university has started functioning a few years back, long run productivity change analysis could not be carried out. This will be a promising area of further research.
3. Full-fledged operation of departments complete in all aspects can provide a clear picture of the efficiency evaluation than the present one.
4. Short duration of time is another constraint for lack of in-depth study of other dimensions like students' performances and their factors.
5. However, despite all these limitations, the study will be an eye opener to the decision-maker at the micro and macro level of the university. This empirical analysis will definitely give right indication of adopting right approach for overall improvement of the performances of the departments and hence, the university. This not only will make the University competitive and efficient but also its rank will find a place where everybody desires to remain in.

Chapter - 5

Education, Farm Production, and Efficiency Overall Summary of the Study

Agriculture is a way of life, a tradition, which for centuries has shaped the thought, the outlook, the culture and the economic life of the people of India. Agriculture, therefore, is and will continue to be the central to all strategies for planned socio-economic development of the country. Rapid growth of agriculture is essential not only to achieve self-reliance at national level but also for household food security and to bring about equity in distribution of income and wealth resulting in rapid reduction in poverty levels. The national policy on agriculture seeks to actualise the vast untapped growth potential of Indian agriculture faster agricultural development, promote value addition, discourage migration to urban areas in search of industrial employment, create employment in rural areas, secure a fair standard of living for the farmers and their families and face the challenges arising out of economic liberalisation and globalisation. Existing low food grain productivity reflects low level of technical, allocative and economic efficiency. In the traditional agriculture, the farmers were adopting the centuries old farm practices what their forefathers were doing. So they were efficient not less than any farm experts. However, the disequilibrium on account of modernisation and commercialisation of agriculture reduced the excessive importance given to land as a factor of production and focused on the efficiency of human capital as it brought differences in the farmer's ability to receive, decode and adopt the new information onto the farm production. Hence, Education of the farm household, as a part of the human capital became a determining factor of differences in the efficiency in the farm production.

Objectives of the Study

1. *Agriculture is the backbone and lifeblood for the people of the state. The strategy for poverty alleviation, reducing the burden of unemployment and improving the standard of the living of the people will be successful only if agriculture transforms. Hence, the first and foremost objective is to emphasise on the* ***role of agriculture in the over all development of the state.***
2. The second most important objective is to emphasise on the **growth in the agricultural production and productivity** to ensure sufficient food grains supply to meet the increasing demand of the growing population and growing urbanisation.
3. To focus on the **role of human capital in general and farmers' education** in terms of the years of schooling completed in particular in improving efficiency and productivity in agricultural production.
4. To make a **quantitative assessment of the effects of farmers' education** in improving the capacity of the farm households in selecting and allocating inputs-mix that improves productivity, improving cost efficiency as well as profit efficiency of the farms under the study area.
5. To establish the link between the farm households in one hand, and the **role of outside agents** (government, Private, NGO, educational institutes, Research institutes) in disseminating farm production related information to the people at grass root level

that directly or indirectly improves the efficiency of the farm households.

6. To stress on **the introduction of agricultural oriented education** in the school and college level for reducing the pressure educational unemployment either through public or through private initiative.

Hypotheses of the Study

In view of the above-mentioned objectives, the following null and corresponding alternative hypotheses are framed and are tested for their statistical significance.

- *Null Hypothesis (Ho)-Average education of the family of the farm household has no significant contribution in farm production.*
- *Null Hypothesis (Ho)- Education of the effective head of the farm household has no effect on the technical efficiency and allocative efficiency in farm production.*
- *Null Hypothesis (Ho)- Cost-minimising efficiency does not improve with the increase in the levels of education of the effective head of the farm household.*
- *Null Hypothesis (Ho)- Average education of the family of the effective head do not have any significant effect on cost efficiency.*
- *Null Hypothesis (Ho)- Total volume of profit earned does not differ significantly with the variation in the educational level of the effective head of the farm household.*
- *Null Hypothesis (Ho)- The profit efficiency of the effective head of the farm households does not vary with the differences in the average education of the family of the farm household of the effective head.*

Nature, Type and Sources of Data

For the purpose of the empirical analysis primary data of the 200 farm households have been collected from the **Goleipur** Panchayat of **Korei** block, Jajpur district, Orissa

(It is renamed as Odisha). The specific area of the study is chosen for four reasons: (1) all the villages of the study area as well as of the Panchayat are located either side of the National Highway No. 5 that extends from **Kolkata to Chennai**, (2) The soil is comparatively more fertile as the river the **Kharashrota,** the tributary of the Brahmani, passes through this area, (3) the entire Panchayat is well connected to the major commercial places such as Jajpur Town, Panikoili, the district headquarter; Jajpur Keonjhar Road, the steel city of Orissa and Chandikhol that connects to the Paradeep sea port, (4) multi-cropping farms. Since the soil is of high quality, the farmers grow multiple of crops, such as, HYV rice, Sugarcane, Groundnut and other vegetables. The rotation of crops not only improves their income but also it upgrades the quality of the soil. Because of the well road connectivity to different market places, the farmers get the advantage of the growing demand for the agricultural product in the market.

A formal permission was taken from the Sarpancha of the Village Panchayat to collect information from the farmers under the study area. Six villages have been purposively selected for collecting information from 200 farm households. Since the villages are very much close to each other, there are no observed differences in the geographical features, cultural practices as well as the farm practices of the people. Whatever technological advancement and new information regarding the modern farm practices are available; it has equal access to all the farm households in the study area. A questionnaire, both in Oriya and English language, has been made in order to make the people convenient in understanding the content of the question and the purpose of the question and to answer the question in an appropriate manner. The entire questionnaire consists of fourteen main questions related to the socio-economic status of the farmers, area production productivity, inputs used, sources of revenue and the cost of inputs. The six villages have been purposively selected for the purpose of collection of primary data for the study. The farm households are randomly chosen irrespective of the caste, class, creed and religion, farm size and economic status.

In addition to the primary survey, data have also been collected from many published sources, such as, Economic Survey of Orissa (various issues), Statistical Handbook of Jajpur District (various issues) and Economic Survey of India (various issues).

The present study has used three different methods in estimating technical and allocative effect of education of the farm people: production function approach; cost function approach and profit function approach. Since the objective is to estimate the effect of education on output, not on profit and cost, a production function of Cobb-Douglas type has been considered and estimated. Single crop production function for each crop with output measured in physical quantities as well as the whole farm production function in terms of gross value. According to Welch, the 'worker effect' can be estimated by specifying an engineering production function for a single crop with education as one of the variable (independent).

Summary of the Results

The parameters of the Cobb-Douglas production function are estimated through the OLS method and the MNVP of education showing technical effect of education for all the three crops have been individually calculated. The primary inputs such as labour power, fertiliser, tractor hour and in some cases the bullock labour are statistically significant in improving the production. The calculated marginal net value product of education for paddy groundnut and sugarcane are respectively Rs 928.97, Rs 724.48 and Rs 263.74. The gross value of output for the farm business as a whole have been estimated to calculate the allocative effect of education. The marginal net value product of education for the farm business as a whole is Rs 2079.43 and the allocative effect is estimated to be Rs 1106.39. The effect of schooling at different levels has been estimated in the form of dummy variable. In general it is concluded that the farmers education above primary and higher primary level has positive and significant impact in improving technical and allocative efficiency. In case of paddy production, the estimated effect of higher secondary and college level education are 6.8 per cent and 5.3 per cent respectively. The average education of the family has also positive and significant effect on improving technical efficiency. In case of groundnut production, the college education has significantly more impact than the high school education (12 per cent and 7.7 per cent). In case of sugarcane, the college level education has positive and significant on the technical efficiency. As far as the average education of the family is concerned it does not have any significant impact on groundnut and sugarcane production. This seems that the family members are more acquainted with the paddy production. Since sugarcane and groundnut require more skills in using fertiliser, irrigation and plantation timing, college level education seems more effective in improving the technical efficiency. The negative impact of primary and upper primary schooling is due to the fact that the knowledge acquired at those levels of schooling is not sufficient to capture the benefit of modern technology and hence, technical efficiency goes down. This has also proved the fact that more levels of schooling dominate over the experience of the farm household.

As far as the coefficients of the frontier cost function are concerned, all the parameters except pesticide price are positive and statistically significant in paddy cost function. It shows the importance of the use of these inputs in paddy production.. The average education of the family shows positive but insignificant effect on the cost inefficiency. The implication is that the more educated family gives least importance to the farming practice and most frequently argues in favour of subsistence production that can fulfill the family need for the food-grains. The experience and the years of schooling of the effective head show positive and statistically significant effect on cost efficiency. The experience of the farm household has significant contribution in reducing cost efficiency, even though; it does not have any significant contribution in technical efficiency. In addition to this, the average education of the effective head, college education dummy (D_1) and high school education dummy (D_2) also play significant role in improving cost efficiency. The farm households having college education are more effective in reducing cost inefficiency than the high school farmers. The estimated gamma value indicates that 75 per cent of the variation in the total paddy cost of production among the paddy farm households is due to the differences in their cost inefficiency.

The log likelihood ratio test for the parameters of the groundnut stochastic cost function shows that the null hypothesis that there is no difference between models with efficiency and without efficiency component stochastic cost frontier is rejected at one per cent level of significance. The Gamma (ã) value of the model is 0.95 implying that 95 per cent of the variations in the costs among the groundnut farmers is due to cost inefficiency and the null hypothesis that (Ho: ã =0) is rejected at 1 per cent level of significance. As far as the inefficiency factors are concerned, all the variables such as education of the family of the effective farm households, experience of the effective farm and the experience of the farm household are statistically significant at 5 per cent level. This supports the result obtained by Ogundary (2002). Again the average education of the effective farm household is used as a dummy factor and the result reveals that the farms having college level education does not contribute significantly in improving the cost efficiency in the groundnut production. However, the effective farm households having high school education (8-10) completed, significantly contribute in reducing cost inefficiency in the groundnut production. The education dummy 3, (primary schooling), even though, reduces cost inefficiency, it is statistically insignificant. Of course, all the farm households adopt almost similar method of production; the differences cost efficiency comes in the actual time the farms have sown the seeds, the preparation of the soil according to the need of the crop etc. For example, some more educated farmers receive the prior information on weather either from the radio or from the newspaper or from television forecasting and accordingly they go on with their cultivation. Whereas, the less educated farmers only follow the leading farm households and do the practice little bit late and that leads to the differences in cost efficiency. Similarly, more educated farmers most often cultivate their land just after cultivation for better soil preparation but some of the farmers hesitate to cultivate in that time just because of the fact that it is a bad month for agriculture from astrological point of view. The most interesting fact is that the more educated farm households take the lead in the adoption in the latest technology in the expectation of getting something more and new. But the first time adoption creates some managerial trouble due to the failure of meeting of all the requirements for the new technology. For example, when the new reaper machines were brought for cutting the crops in less cost and less time, it was realised in the field that the machine couldn't run smoothly because of uncouthness of the surface of the soil. Secondly, the machine requires that all the plants to be cut must stand straight. This results in some kind of delay and double use of human labour and wastage. Another instance is that some farmers also try new seeds with shortest duration. However, lack of complete scientific process of cultivation leads to low productivity and higher cost.

Preparatory tillage is very important operation in sugarcane cultivation. Sugarcane roots penetrate up to 90 centimeters deep in the soil and, hence, for better growth tillage has an important effect. Soil preparation must destroy the stumps of the old canes and improve any bad physical soil characteristics or loss of structure those have developed during the previous year. In this background it can be argued that the importance of both bullock driven plough wood tilling and tractor tilling is very much prominent. The use of fertiliser such as nitrogen, potash and phosphorous and irrigation is utmost essential. This in fact is revealed from the results of the statistically significant beta coefficients of the sugarcane frontier cost function of the study area.

The model without inefficiency components is tested against the model with efficiency components and the null hypothesis that there is no difference between these two models is rejected at one per cent level of significance. The likelihood function value for without inefficiency component is 101.78 and the corresponding value for the alternative is 347.59. From the gamma value (ã), it is concluded that 97 per cent of the inefficiency is due to the cost inefficiency which is attributed to education of the family of the effective head of the household, experience of the effective head of the household and the education of the effective head. All these factors, of course, contribute positively in reducing cost inefficiency, the differences comes when the education of the effective head is used as a dummy variable for college education, high school education and primary schooling. In this case dummy 1 is statistically significant in reducing the cost inefficiency in the sugarcane production. Since sugarcane production takes 16 to 18 months, lots of care has to be taken by the farmers. For example, preparation of the soil suited for plantation; preparation of plant cuttings and culture of plant cuttings, use of proper dose of fertiliser in appropriate time; choice of irrigation method such as, flood irrigation and drip irrigation. It has also been realised that the farmers with more schooling specially college level are more prone to better management with efficient method of production as stated above, many farmers use drip irrigation which saves 30 to 40 per cent of the water and also thereby the diesel and electricity consumption also reduces accordingly. On the other side, the farmers with little education, of course, have contribution but not statistically significant. Some time the wrong choice of using bullock labour instead of tractor for initial cultivation reduces cost efficiency.

As far as the cost efficiency scores for all the three crops are concerned, the average cost efficiency scores for paddy, groundnut and sugarcane are, 1.130, 1.160 and 1.365 respectively. It means that farmers are quite familiar with paddy cultivation since it is the farming that the farmers do it from the inception of agriculture. On the other hand, the farm households face lot of difficulties in adopting the best farming practices for groundnut and sugarcane. Frequently, the farmers face the trouble of getting genetically tested crops; identifying the pest that affect the crops and use of suitable pesticides; and the difficulties of getting fertilizer. In addition to this, timing of showing season; cultivation method, identification of soil quality play very important role in reducing the cost of production in these two crops. Hence, higher education plays a spectacular role in reducing cost inefficiency.

The maximum likelihood estimates of the parameters of the profit function and the inefficiency function are jointly estimated by using the FRONTIER 4.1c (Coelli, 1996). The coefficients of labour price, bullock labor price, fertilizer price and tractor hour price have shown the negative and statistically significant sign as it is expected theoretically. However, the coefficients of the pesticide price and manures price do not have significant impact in reducing gross margin of the farm household in paddy production. As far as the inefficiency components are concerned, the average education of the effective farm households, education dummy D_1 (college education) and D_2 (high school education) have positive impact in improving profit efficiency of the paddy-growing farmers.

As far as the coefficients of the parameters of the profit frontier function for groundnut are concerned, the coefficient of the size of the land is positive and statistically significant.

One-acre increase in the land raises the profit margin by 8.2 per cent. As it has been shown that the share of labor expenditure in the total cost of groundnut production on an average is 63.9 per cent, it clearly reveals the fact that human labour still constitutes an important factor input for the groundnut production. The coefficient of price of the labour power is negative and statistically significant. As far as the coefficient of bullock labour price is concerned it is positive and statistically significant. The coefficients fertilizer price, irrigation price and tractor hour price are negatively significant. It should be mentioned that the bullock labour expenditure in the groundnut cost of production is around 15 per cent and tractor hour expenditure is 12 per cent. This implies that there is high substitutability between these two factors. High bullock labour price forces the farmers to use more of tractor power, which improves the margin gross margin of the farmer. In inefficiency function, the average education of the effective head of the household, average education of family has positive and significant contribution in improving the profit efficiency margin of the farm household. It has been observed that more experienced farmers are generally from old generation and are very much pessimistic about the adoption of the latest technology. Their over all roles in improving profit efficiency are negligible. The most important factor that reduces profit inefficiency is college education dummy (D_1) and high school education dummy (D_2).

The MLE results of the coefficients of the sugarcane profit frontier and the coefficients of the inefficiency functions show that the coefficients of the land area, price of labour, price of nitrogen (urea), price of potash, calcium, price of tractor hour and price of irrigation hour are statistically significant and take the sign as expected. However, the price of Super and price of manure are not statistically significant. In the inefficiency components the coefficients of family education, average education of the farmers and the education dummy D_1 and D_2 are positive and statistically significant. It shows the fact that farmer's education above primary and higher primary levels have significant contribution in improving profit efficiency of the sugarcane farmers. Ninety-three per cent of the total differences in the inefficiency are due to profit inefficiency. Lastly, the null hypothesis that there is no difference between the profit efficiency model without inefficiency components and profit frontier with efficiency components is rejected. As far as the mean profit efficiency is concerned, it is lowest in sugarcane production (79%) and highest in the groundnut production (93%).

Conclusion of the Study

From the entire analysis it can be concluded that in addition to the basic agricultural inputs, the education of the farmer, education of the family and experience do have significant role as it has been emphasised by Schultz (1964). However, the primary and upper primary schooling has no significant contribution in reducing either technical, cost or profit inefficiency. Since most of the schools provide formal education with theoretical knowledge, the students after the completion of the course do not find any use of application to the practical field. The curriculum of the general courses is just to get certificates. Being agriculturally dominated, the school and college education must provide the farming courses, which can equip the students to know and understand the techniques of cultivation, the procedures of cultivation and the ways of scientific cultivation with practical experience. This not only saves the students being unproductive and unemployed after the completion of education, but also the participation of more educated people in agriculture will increase. As a result, the pressure of educated people on getting employment in the industry and service sector will diminish and the influx of large section of the rural unemployed youth to the urban areas will get reduced. Once the educated people will choose agriculture as an occupation, it will be commercialised and there will be a tremendous change in the farming practice that the existing farmers have been adopting. Since majority of the people are dependent on agriculture and land is the most important assets for the rural people, the cropping pattern and intensity of the pattern will change and ultimately the standard of living of the people will improve and the economic status of the state will see an upward trend.

To achieve the objectives of National Agricultural policy investment in the farm people in terms of education is utmost important. The government should introduce the farm management oriented education in all school and college level education. The course curriculum should contain the lessons of crop management and the methods of cultivation. The students should be allowed to do the project work on agricultural practices. Along with this, the government should take initiative in setting up special colleges for farm management in different blocks. In addition to these private organisations NGOs must come forward in providing these facilities at grass root level. Different types of agricultural exhibitions showing latest technology, different machines and pest management practices, must have to be arranged at school and college levels so that it will directly and indirectly help in higher growth in agricultural production. Since the government at state and central level is spending lot of money on Sarva Siksha Abhiyan (Education for All), a strong and serious effort in providing farming education should be made at all level, starting from village to state level. The so called Gram Sewaks (government extension agent) at each panchayat level must be made accountable to the people of that area and must provide the details of all information on farming practices at the schools in each village, so that the knowledge created in the laboratory will be delivered to the farming practice. **Hence, the educational system should change into farming oriented and some top 'A' schools (Agricultural Schools) in the line of top 'B' schools** should be set up so that the long cherished desire of converting the state into Ram Rajya (as dreamt by Mahatma Gandhi,

The Father of Nation) will be realised. Therefore, Education in general and farm-oriented education in practical should be the main instrument of making a transformation in the agrarian system.

References

1. Aigner, D.J., C.A.K. Lovell and P. Schmidt (1977), Formulation and estimation of stochastic frontier production function models, Journal of Econometrics, 6(1), 21-37.
2. Altbach, P.G., L. Reisberg and L.E. Rumbley (2010), Tracking a Global Academic Revolution, Change, March/ April, 30-39.
3. Andersen, P. and Petersen, N. C. (1993), A procedure for ranking efficient units in data envelopment, Analysis Management Science, 39(10), 1261-1294.
4. Athanassopoulos, A.D. and Shale, E. (1997), Assessing the comparative efficiency of higher education institutions in the UK by means of data envelopment analysis, Education Economics, 5, 117-134.
5. Arrow, K. (1973), Higher education as a lter, Journal of Public Economics, 2 (3), 193-216.
6. Banker, R.D., Charnes, A. and Cooper, W.W. (1984), Some models for estimating technical and scale inefficiencies in data envelopment analysis, Management Science, 30, 1078-1092.
7. Banker, R., and Morey, R. (1986), Effciency analysis for exogenous xed inputs and outputs. Operations Research, 34, 513-21.
8. Becker, Gary S. (1975), Human Capital, Chicago: University of Chicago Press.
9. Beasley, J. E. (1990), Comparing university departments, OMEGA Journal of Management Science, 18, 171-83.

10. Beasley, J.E. (1995), Determining teaching and research efficiencies, Journal of the Operational Research Society, 46, 441-452.
11. Brennan, S., Haelermans, C., and Ruggiero, J. (2013), Non parametric estimation of education productivity incorporating nondiscretionary inputs with an application to Dutch schools. European Journal of Operational Research, 234, 809–818.
12. Bridge, R., Judd, C., and Moock, P. (1979), The determinants of educational outcomes. Cambridge, MA: Ballinger.
13. Carnevale, A.P., Smith, N., and Strohl, J. (2010), Help Wanted: Projections of Jobs and Education Requirements Through 2018. Georgetown University Center on Education and the Workforce. Available:http://www9.georgetown.edu/grad/gppi/hpi/cew/pdfs/HelpWanted.FullReport.pdf [July 2012].
14. Charnes, A., Cooper, W.W. and Rhodes, E. (1978), Measuring the efficiency of decision-making units, European Journal of Operational Research, 2, 429-444.
15. Chellaraj, G., K.E. Maskus and A. Mattoo (2005), The Contribution of Skilled Immigration and International Graduate Students to U.S. Innovation, World Bank Policy Research Working Paper 3588.
16. CERI (2009), Higher Education to 2030, Vol. 2. Globalisation, OECD, Paris.
17. Cohn, E., and Geske, T. (1990), The economics of education. Oxford, England: Pergamon.
18. Cooper, W.W., Lawrence, M. S., and Tone K. (2000, 2005), Data Envelopment Analysis: A Comprehensive Text with Models, Applications References and DEA Solver Software, Kluwer Academic Publisher, New York.
19. Coleman, J.S. (1966), Equality of Educational Opportunity, Washington, DC:US GPO.

20. Dantzig, G.B.(1951), Maximisation of a linear function of variables subject to linear inequalities, in T.C. Koopmans (ed.), Activity Analysis of Production and Allocation, New York: Wiley.
21. Deem, R. (2001), Globalisation, New Managerialism, Academic Capitalism and Entrepreneurialism in Universities: Is the Local Dimension Still Important?, Comparative Education, 37(1): 7-20.
22. Dolton, P.J. (1985), Signaling and screening in the graduate labour market, Hull Economic Research Paper no.123.
23. Deller, S.C. and Rudnicki, E.R. (1993), Production efficiency in elementary education: The case of Maine public schools, Economics of Education Review, 12, 45-57.
24. Essid, H., Ouellette, P., and Vigeant, S. (2014), Productivity, effciency and technical change of Tunisian schools: A bootstrapped Malmquist Approach with Quasi-xed Inputs, Omega, 42, 88-97.
25. Europa (2006), Delivering on the Modernisation Agenda for Universities: Education, Research and Innovation, Communication to the Council and the European Parliament, (COM) 2006 208, nal, European Commission, Brussels.
26. Fa ¨re, R., Grosskopf, S., and Weber, W. (1989), Measuring school district performance. Public Finance Quarterly, 17, 409-428.
27. Farrell, M.J. (1957), The measurement of productive efficiency, Journal of the Royal Statistical Society, Series A (General), 120, 253-289.
28. Førsund, F.R., C.A.K. Lovell and P. Schmidt (1980), A survey of frontier production functions and of their relationship to effciency measurement, Journal of Econometrics, 13, 5-25.

29. Friedman, Milton and Kuznets, Simon. (1946), Income from Independent Professional Practice, Cambridge, MA: NBER.

30. Haelermans, C., De Witte, K., and Blank, J. L. T. (2012), On the allocation of resources for secondary schools, Economics of Education Review, 31(5), 575-586.

31. Haelermans, C., and Ruggiero, J. (2013), Estimating technical and allocative effciency in the public sector: A nonparametric analysis of Dutch Schools, European Journal of Operational Research, 227(1), 174-181.

32. Haveman, Robert and Barbara Wolfe (1984), Schooling and economic well being: the role of non-market effects, The Journal of Human Resources, 19 (3), 377-407.

33. Hanushek, E.(1986), The economics of schooling: Production and efficiency in public schools, Journal of Economic Literature, 24, 1141-1177.

34. Hanushek, A.E. (1979), Conceptual and empirical issues in the estimation of educational production functions, Journal of Human Resources, 14, 351-88.

35. Hazelkorn, E. and A. Moynihan (2010), Transforming Academic Practice: Human Resources Challenges, in S. Kyvik and B. Lepori (eds) The Research Mission of Higher Education Institutes Outside the University Sector, Springer, Dordrecht, 77-96.

36. Hutton, W. (2006), 'Building Successful Cities in the Knowledge Economy: The Role of "Soft Policy" Instruments, OECD.

37. Johnes, G. and Johnes, J. (1993), Measuring the research performance of UK economics departments: An application of data envelopment analysis, Oxford Economic Papers, 45, 332-347.

38. Johnes, J. and Johnes, G. (1995), Research funding and performance in U.K. university departments of economics: A frontier analysis, Economics of Education Review, 14, 301-314.

39. Johnes, J. (2006) Data Envelopment analysis and its application to the measurement of efficiency in higher education, Economics of Education Review, 25, 273-288.

40. Johnson, A., and Ruggiero, J. (2011), Nonparametric measurement of productivity and efficiency in education. Annals of Operations Research. doi:10.1007/s10479-011-0880-9.

41. Jondrow, J., C.A.K., Lovell, I. S. Materou and P. Schmidt, (1982), On the estimation of technical inffeciency in the stochastic frontier production function model', Journal of Econometrics, 19, 233-8.

42. Leibenstein, H. (1966), Allocative efficiency vs. X-efficiency. American Economic Review, 56, 392-415.

43. Lovell, C.A.K. (1993), Production frontiers and productive eciency, in H.O. Fried, C.A.K. Lovell and S.S. Schmidt (eds), The Measurement of Productive Efficiency, Oxford: Oxford University Press, 3-67.

44. Maddison, A. (1991), Dynamic Forces of Capitalist Development, Oxford: Oxford University Press.

45. Marginson, S. and M. van der Wende (2007), 'Globalisation and Higher Education', OECD Education Working Papers No. 8, OECD, Paris.

46. McCarty, T., and Yaisawarng, S. (1993), Technical efficiency in New Jersey School Districts. In H. O. Fried, C. A. K. Lovell, and S. S. Schmidt (Eds.), The measurement of productive efciency (271-287). New York: Oxford University Press.

47. McMahon, Walter W. (1987), 'Externalities in education', in George Psacharopoulos (ed.), Economics of Education; Research and Studies, Oxford and New York: Pergamon Press.

48. Madden, G., Savage, S. and Kemp, S. (1997), Measuring public sector efficiency: A study of economics departments at Australian universities, Education Economics, 5, 153-168.

49. Marshall, Alfred ([1890] 1961), The Principles of Economics, London: Macmillan.

50. Mayston, D.J. (1996), Educational attainment and resource use: Mystery or econometric misspecification? Education Economics 4, 127-142.

51. Migue´, J., and Be ´langer, G. (1974), Towards a general theory of 67. Santiago, P., K. Tremblay, E. Basri and E. Arnal (2008), Tertiary Education for the Knowledge Society, 2, OECD, Paris.

68. Schmidt, P. (1985–6), Frontier production functions, Econometric Reviews, 4(2), 289-328.

69. Schultz, T.W. (1961), Investment in human capital, American Economic Review, 51, 1-17.

70. Sengupta, J.K. (1999), The measurement of dynamic productive efficiency, Bulletin of Economic Research, 51(2), 111-24.

71. Sengupta, J.K. and Sfeir, R.E. (1986), Production frontier estimates of scale in public schools in California, Economics of Education Review, 5, 297-307.

72. Sinuany-Stern, Z., Mehrez, A. and Barboy, A. (1994), Academic departments efficiency via DEA, Computers and Operations Research, 21, 543-556.

73. Smith, A. ([1776] 1991), The Wealth of Nations, New York: Alfred A. Knop

74. Smith, P. and Mayston, D. (1987), Measuring efficiency in the public sector, OMEGA Journal of Management Science, 15, 181-189.

75. Spence, M.A. (1973), Job market signalling, Quarterly Journal of Economics, 87, 355-74.

76. Stevens, P. and Weale, M. (2004), Education and Economic Growth Chapter 4. pp. 164-188 in the Book Handbook on the Economics of Education (Eds) Johnes G. and Jill Johns (Edward Elgar Publishing Limited, UK.

77. Stiglitz, J.E. (1975), The theory of "screening", education, and the distribution of income, American Economic Review, 65 (3), 283-300.
78. Strumilin, S.G. (1924), Khoziaistvennoe znachenie narodnovo obrazovaniia, (Economic signicance of national education), Planovoe Khoziaistvo, 9-10, translated and reprinted in English in UNESCO (1968), Readings in the Economics of Education, Paris: UNESCO, 413-52.
79. Tone, K. (1997), DEA with controllable category levels in proceedings of the 1997 Spring National Conference of the Operation Research Society of Japan, 126-27.
80. Tone, K. (2001), Slacks-based measure of efficiency in data envelopment analysis, European Journal of Operational Research, 130, 489-509.
81. van der Werf, M. (2009), Researcher Officers Unusually Candid Description of University's Effort to Rise in Rankings, Chronicle of Higher Education, 3 June.
82. Walsh, J. R. (1935), Capital concept applied to man, Quarterly Journal of Economics, 49 (2), 284-5.
83. Wolfe, Barbara and R. Haveman (2001), Accounting for the social and non-market benefits of education, in John Helliwell (ed.), The Contribution of Human and Social Capital to Sustained Economic Growth and Well Being, Paris: OECD.
84. Worthington, Andrew (2001), An empirical survey of frontier efficiency measurement techniques in education, Education Economics, 9, 3, pp. 245-268.

Appendix –A

Table A1: Descriptive Statistics of the Input-Output (Case-2)

	Area	*No. of perm fac*	*total expen-diture*	*No. of female student*	*No. of male*	*Total score*	*Avg marks*	*First Div*
Max	11490	7	21325304	29	20	535	129	25
Min	3000	2	2050046.	1	0	58	55	1
Average	5327.92	4.28	9933545.	11.16	6.76	206.96	69.76	11.6
SD	2330.177	1.510	5558452.	7.297561	4.347689	132.032	17.05642	6.811755

Table A2: Correlation matrix of Inputs and outputs (Case-2)

Items	*1st case*		*2nd case*		*3rd case*	
	CCR	*BCC*	*CCR*	*BCC*	*CCR*	*BCC*
Rank (score)	23(1.30)	20(1.06)	21(1.28)	21(1.131)	12(1.21)	1(1)
Reference Group	Pcm-2.96, zool-28.85, math-10.21, hind-76.25, edu-10.53	Hort-27.61, geol-44.11, psy-1.57, edu-24.03, masc-2.66	Pcm-6.3, zool-37.82, hind-79.88, edu-8.2	Zool-32.57, phy-11.89, hist-47.57, edu-7.9	Zool-1.95, hind-24.52	
Inputs/ outputs	5, 3, 27	5, 3, 27	5, 3, 25	5, 3, 25	5, 2, 22	5, 2, 22
projection	30.02 each	10.38, 6.48, 6.48	28.20 each	18.97, 13.14, 13.14	63.67, 21.58	
Weighted data	11.37, 22.57, 66.05	0(3.89), 99.79, 0.02	9.5, 22.8, 66.6	0, 87.37, 12.62	0 (66.49), 1,	0, 1
RTS		DRS		DRS		DRS

Appendix-B

Table B1: Descriptive Statistics of Inputs and Outputs (Case-3)

	Area	*No. of perm fac*	*Total expenditure*	*No. of female student*	*No. of male*	*Total score*	*Avg marks*
Max	12500	11	20500468	28	20	535	142
Min	3100	3	3758419.1	4	1	79	57
Average	6392.227	5.181818	11494927	13.27273	8.227273	239.2273	82.43636
SD	2891.929	1.849726	4412739.4	7.484419	4.591809	125.9863	30.36641

Table B2: Correlation Matrix (Case-4)

	Area	*No. of perm fac*	*Total expenditure*	*No. of female student*	*No. of male*	*Total score*	*Avg marks*
Area	1	0.767624	0.155250	0.12482	0.74473	-0.05748	0.69007
No. of perm fac	0.767624	1	0.278930	0.45936	0.78717	0.14552	0.54725
total expenditure	0.15525	0.278931	1	0.55352	0.33449	0.17537	0.09630
No. of female student	0.124829	0.459365	0.553520	1	0.24684	-0.02908	0.21523
No. of male	0.74473	0.787176	0.334496	0.24684	1	0.09569	0.63039
Total score	-0.057486	0.145525	0.175375	-0.02908	0.09569	1	-0.24523
Avg marks	0.690075	0.547251	0.096302	0.21523	0.63039	-0.24523	1

Index